AN EARLY IRISH READER

AN
EARLY IRISH READER

BY

N. KERSHAW CHADWICK

*Associate of Newnham College, Cambridge; formerly
Lecturer in the University of St Andrews*

CAMBRIDGE

AT THE UNIVERSITY PRESS

1927

To
M. D. BRINDLEY
and
E. E. H. WELSFORD

CAMBRIDGE UNIVERSITY PRESS
Cambridge, New York, Melbourne, Madrid, Cape Town,
Singapore, São Paulo, Delhi, Tokyo, Mexico City

Cambridge University Press
The Edinburgh Building, Cambridge CB2 8RU, UK

Published in the United States of America by Cambridge University Press, New York

www.cambridge.org
Information on this title: www.cambridge.org/9781107633421

First published 1927
First paperback edition 2011

A catalogue record for this publication is available from the British Library

ISBN 978-1-107-63342-1 Paperback

PREFACE

The *Scél Mucci Mic Dathó*, or "Story of Mac Dathó's Pig," is justly regarded as one of the best of the Irish Sagas. In spite of its brevity it is very varied in character, and several different types of prose and poetry are represented in it. It is well adapted therefore to serve as an introduction to the study of Early Irish Literature in the original, and for this purpose the present Reader is primarily intended.

The text which follows is taken from the Book of Leinster; but all the existing MSS., with the exception of the modernised version in H. 6. 8 (Trinity College, Dublin), have been consulted, including the unpublished Harl. 5280, of which I have made a transcript. By the kind permission of Professor Watson of Edinburgh who allowed me to consult his transcript, I have been enabled to examine MS. Edinburgh XXXVI. Unfortunately my book had already gone to Press, and it has therefore not been possible for me to do more than insert one or two notes on this MS. in my introduction. The text, which is in the nature of a modern paraphrase, is of considerable interest. I have therefore added a note at the conclusion of the book indicating the principal points in which it differs from the other MSS.

The vocabulary has been made very full, and contains all the words and most of the forms which occur in the text. It is based in the main on Windisch's invaluable *Wörterbuch*. I have also made use of his Glossary to the *Táin Bó Cúalnge*, and of W. Stokes' and K. Meyer's *Archiv für celtische Lexikographie*, and Meyer's supplement, *Contributions to Irish Lexicography*, as well as the vocabulary in Strachan's *Stories from the Táin*, and *Selections from the Old Irish Glosses*, and the Glossary to Atkinson's *Passions and Homilies*, O'Donovan's supplement to O'Reilly's *Dictionary*, and Dinneen's *Dictionary of Modern Irish*.

The Index of Proper Names is intended primarily to direct elementary students to the principal stories in which the heroes mentioned in our saga figure prominently. The references, which are in no sense exhaustive, are only given to such books or periodicals as are readily accessible. Such references are given where possible to English translations, but it will be found that in most cases these are accompanied by the Irish text.

On the same severely practical principle references are given where possible to grammars which are easily accessible in English and which do not demand a philological training on the part of the student, such as Windisch's *Kurzgefasste irische Grammatik*

(English translation by Norman Moore, Cambridge, 1882), Strachan, *Old-Irish Paradigms*[2] (Dublin, 1909), O'Connell, *Grammar of Old Irish* (Belfast, 1912); also to Dottin, *Manuel d'Irlandais moyen* (Paris, 1913). Pokorny's *Old Irish Grammar* (Dublin, 1914), his *Altirische Grammatik* (Leipzig, 1925), and his *Historical Reader of Old Irish* (Halle, 1923) are more recent books which will be found specially helpful to students who know Latin and Greek, and who have some knowledge of Indo-European Philology. More advanced students, who read German, will be in a position to consult Thurneysen, *Handbuch des Altirischen*, I. *Grammatik* etc. (Heidelberg, 1909) and Pedersen, *Vergleichende Grammatik der keltischen Sprachen* (Göttingen, 1913).

My warmest thanks are due to Professor T. Ó'Máille of Galway and Professor J. Fraser of Oxford. Professor Ó'Máille has very kindly read the proofs of my text, translation and notes, and I have to thank him for many corrections and additions, especially in the notes. Although I was not known to him personally he generously placed the resources of his learning and research at my disposal, and it is a matter of sincere regret to me that the scope of the book, intended as it is primarily for beginners, did not permit me to incorporate all the illuminating material, especially the references, which he put before me.

To Professor Fraser I am under heavy obligations. Though he also was unacquainted with me he most kindly consented to read all my proofs, including the vocabulary. He has saved me from many pitfalls, and has been most ungrudging in the help he has given me. His corrections, suggestions and criticisms have been of the greatest possible value to me. I need hardly add that I alone am responsible for the many shortcomings which still remain. In preparing an Early Irish Saga for the use of beginners I realise only too well that I am venturing on peculiarly dangerous ground.

I have also to thank Miss J. Young of Girton College who kindly compared my transcript of the text with the original MS. of the Book of Leinster in the Library of Trinity College, Dublin. To Miss A. Walsh, Inspector of Schools, Dublin, to Miss J. Walsh, Lecturer in the Cambridge Training College for Women Graduates, and to my pupil, Miss A. M. D. Hoare, I am indebted for various kind services. Lastly I wish to thank the Syndics of the University Press for undertaking the publication of the book, and the staffs of the University Press and of the University Library for their unfailing courtesy and help while the work was in progress.

TABLE OF CONTENTS

AN EARLY IRISH READER

INTRODUCTION

The story of Mac Dathó's Pig is found in six Manuscripts.

(1) The earliest is the Book of Leinster (LL., fo. 111b), which was written c. 1160 and of which a transcript was edited by Robert Atkinson and published in Dublin in 1880. This MS. is now in the library of the Royal Irish Academy, Dublin (H. 2. 18).

(2) A vellum codex (Rawl. B. 512, fo. 105), written by various hands in the fourteenth and fifteenth centuries[1], and preserved now in the Bodleian Library at Oxford.

(3) A vellum quarto (Harl. 5280, fo. 50), written in the first half of the sixteenth century, and now preserved in the British Museum.

(4) A MS., chiefly vellum (H. 3. 18), dating from the fifteenth or sixteenth century, now in the Library of Trinity College, Dublin. Our text is included in the paper portion of the MS. (p. 743 ff.).

(5) A paper MS. (no. XXXVI, p. 86a), written in 1690–1691, preserved in the National Library of Scotland (formerly the Advocates' Library)[2].

(6) A paper MS. (H. 6. 8, p. 37), preserved in the Library of Trinity College, Dublin.

The text in LL. was published by Windisch in *Irische Texte mit Wörterbuch* at Leipzig in 1880, with variant readings from Harl. 5280 and H. 3. 18 in footnotes. The text in Harl. 5280 has never been published in full. An account of the Manuscript will be found in O'Grady and Flower, *Catalogue of Irish Manuscripts in the British Museum*, Vol. II (London, 1926), p. 298 ff. The text of H. 3. 18 was published by A. M. Scarre in *Anecdota from Irish MSS.* (Halle, 1913). The version in Rawlinson B. 512 was published with a translation by K. Meyer in *Hibernica Minora*

---

[1] See Stokes, *Tripartite Life of Patrick* (Rolls Series, 1887), Vol. I, p. xiv.
[2] See Mackinnon, *A Descriptive Catalogue of Gaelic Manuscripts in the Advocates' Library, Edinburgh*, etc. (Edinburgh, 1912), p. 144.

(*Anecdota Oxoniensia*, Oxford, 1894). The texts Edin. XXXVI and H. 6. 8 have never been published so far as I am aware, nor do they appear to have been collated or even examined by editors. Mackinnon in his *Descriptive Catalogue of Gaelic Manuscripts in the Advocates' Library, Edinburgh* (Edinburgh, 1912, p. 144) describes the former as an abridged version with many modernisms and corruptions[1]. H. 6. 8 is also a much modernised version which does not contain the poetry.

Besides Meyer's translation of Rawl. B. 512, several translations have been made of Windisch's text from LL. Of these the earliest known to me is a French one by Duvau in the *Revue Archéologique*, Vol. VIII, 1886, p. 336 ff., reprinted by D'Arbois de Jubainville in *L'épopée celtique en Irlande*, p. 66. The translation is very free, and in places approximates rather to a paraphrase, not always in close relation to the text. A German translation which keeps much closer to the text, and which is regarded by Irish scholars as leaving little to be desired, was published by Thurneysen in *Sagen aus dem alten Irland* (Berlin, 1901), p. 1 ff. Thurneysen translates Windisch's text from LL., occasionally however adopting the readings of Harl. 5280 and H. 3. 18 in preference to those of LL. An English translation was published by Leahy in *Heroic Romances of Ireland* (London, 1905), p. 37 ff. Leahy's translation is so close in the main to that of Thurneysen that it appears for the most part to be rather a translation of the German than of the Irish text. Occasionally however he gives an independent rendering, and he was evidently familiar with the original. A scholarly French translation was published by G. Dottin in *L'Épopée Irlandaise* (Paris, 1926), p. 67 ff. The fullest account of the saga, together with a summary of the story and full references to the literature, will be found in Thurneysen, *Die irische Helden- und Königsage* (Halle, 1921), p. 494 ff. The story as told in the ancient MSS. is paraphrased in the Modern Irish *Mac Dathó* by T. Ó'Máille (Dublin, 1924).

No attempt has as yet been made at a comparative study of the MSS. or a critical study of the text, both of which are much

---

[1] No account is taken here of the Scotch MS., but see Preface, p. v, and p. 54 ff. below.

needed. H. 3. 18 and Harl. 5280 are closer to one another than to LL., while Rawl. B. 512 and Edin. XXXVI appear to be more closely related to one another than to the former group. Moreover, Rawl. B. 512 stands somewhat apart from the others in character. Its variants appear to me to be in the nature of changes which have been introduced deliberately by the scribe, and are chiefly of an explanatory character. In accordance with a manifest desire to make his text intelligible to his audience he, or perhaps his authority, whether written or oral, frequently eliminates infixed pronouns and abandons archaic words for more modern forms, *e.g.* the substitution of *lebaid* for *imdai* in ch. 2. Sometimes he resorts to the method dear to scribes of putting the modern equivalent beside the old word. A particularly striking example of his method is his attempt (erroneous, as I believe) to elucidate the *cloendiburgun*, etc., of LL. in ch. 17 into the passage indicating the stoning of Conall, which I have quoted from Rawl. in my note on the passage.

Occasionally the saga teller or the scribe, whichever was responsible, added interesting details not found in the other texts, *e.g.* the defaulting of the Ultonians with regard to Ferloga's *cepóc* (ch. 20) and the part played by Cúrói Mac Dári, cf. note on *Is ...fremaib* in ch. 18 below. The latter instance is of especial interest as it suggests that the scribe was familiar with another tradition in which Cúrói played a part in the story and perhaps obtained the champion's portion (cf. p. 51 below). The phrase used—"Others say"—may mean no more than "Other sources indicate"; but the more natural interpretation is to suppose that another tradition in oral form persisted alongside the written one. It is not unlikely that such oral tradition persisted in ancient, as it does in modern, Ireland[1]. In general however the variations in the MSS. are clearly variations of text. The story is virtually the same in all, and there can be little doubt that all go back to a common original.

---

[1] See Windisch, *Irische Texte, Táin Bó Cúalnge*, p. lix; cf. however Thurneysen, *Irische Helden- und Königsage*, p. 73 f. Heusler has suggested (*Abhandlung der k. preuss. Akad. der Wiss. zu Berlin*, 1913, Phil-Hist. Classe, no. 9, p. 72) that oral tradition influenced the texts of Icelandic sagas some time after they had been committed to writing. A fuller study of the relationship of the poems to the prose texts in the Irish sagas as a whole may throw some light on this subject.

The question of the relationship of the poems[1] to the prose
text of our saga is one of considerable interest owing to the
wide differences shown by the various texts in this respect. In
chs. 1 and 17, Rawl. B. 512 and Ed. XXXVI insert poems not
found in the other versions. These MSS. omit the dialogue poem
in ch. 3 which is included in LL., H. 3. 18, and Harl. 5280, quot-
ing however the first line to indicate its existence. The rhetorics
in ch. 15 are included in all texts except Ed. (cf. p. 55); but
a poem which is attached to the saga after ch. 20 in LL. and
H. 3. 18, and which occurs also in Harl. 5280, is not found in Rawl.
B. 512 or Ed. Thurneysen notes[2] that it is by a different author
from the saga and does not really belong to it. It consists of a
catalogue of the heroes who took part in the fight, including the
names of some heroes who have not been mentioned in the saga,
and differing from the latter in some details. Harl. 5280 adds
after this a poem which appears independently of the saga in
at least two other MSS.,[3] viz. Y.B.L. fo. 259, 2 b (after the Dindsenchas of Mag Lena; cf. p. 5 below), and Laud 610, fo. 58 v, a.
The Laud text was published by Meyer in the Zeitschrift für
celtische Philologie, Vol. III, p. 36; the text in Harl. 5280 by
Windisch in Irische Texte, I, p. 108, immediately after our saga.
This poem is quite short, consisting of only twelve lines. It tells
in summary form the outline of the story, stressing the early
life and remarkable diet of the pig, naming Mesgegra and
Mesroeda as the two Mac Dathó, and representing all the five
provinces of Ireland as taking part in the chase for the hound
Ailbe. The prose note which follows the poem in Laud 610 states
that 300 of the men of Connaught were slain in the hostel of
Mac Dathó, and fifty of the Ulstermen, and that Ailbe was killed
by Ailill's charioteer.

There is evidence that the Scél Mucci Mic Dathó was known
earlier than LL. It is probably the "Destruction of Mac Dathó"

---

[1] For a discussion of metrics and Early Irish rhymed poems the reader is
referred to Kuno Meyer's Primer of Irish Metrics (Dublin, 1909) and his paper on
Learning in Ireland in the Fifth Century and the Transmission of Letters (Dublin,
1913). See also Thurneysen, Zeitschrift für celtische Philologie, Vol. XI, p. 34 ff.

[2] Helden- und Königsage, p. 498 f.

[3] See Thurneysen, Helden- und Königsage, p. 498. This poem and the preceding
one are printed by Windisch immediately after the saga, ed. cit. p. 106 ff.

(*Argain mic Dathó*,) referred to elsewhere in LL. (fo. 151 a) in the list of "primary stories" (*primscéla*)[1] which it was the custom for the *file* or "poet" of ancient Ireland to relate to kings and chiefs. A further reference to Mac Dathó and the pig occurs in ll. 6, 7 of a poem in the Yellow Book of Lecan (fo. 125 a), which is attributed in the title in the MS. to Flannacán mac Cellaigh, who is said to have been slain by the Norsemen in 896[2].

A mnemonic poem enumerating the "halls" (*bruidne*) occurs in MS. H. 1. 17 ff. 7[b], 8[a] and is published with an English translation by Stokes in the *Revue Celtique*, Vol. XXI, p. 396 f. A better copy of this poem is found in Harl. 5280 on fo. 49 b, *i.e.* immediately before our saga. Flower, *op. cit.* p. 315, believes the poem to be a versification of the prose note on the *bruidne* in the *Scél Mucci Mic Dathó*. The story is clearly referred to in ll. 6, 7:

The hostel of Mac dá thó—strong noise, whither came the men of Erin: Together they consumed the swine and carried off the hound Ailbe[3].

The list however differs in several details from the passage in our saga, and I think it more likely that the latter is based on some poetical original similar to, or possibly a variant of, the poem referred to above (cf. note in ch. 1, s.v. *secht n-*).

Two further references occur in the Rennes *Dindsenchas*. In the *Dindsenchas of Mag Lena* we are told how Lena, the son of Mesroeda, found Mac Dathó's pig in the oakwood and reared it for seven years, till just before Mac Dathó's Feast the pig buried him alive in the earth which it grubbed up over him as he lay asleep. Thereupon Follscaide, Mac Dathó's swineherd, bore it off to his master[4]. In the *Dindsenchas of Carman* this same Lena, "son of Mesroeda," is represented as carrying off seven cows from Eochaid Bélbuide. His mother is said to have been "Ucha, wife of Mesgegra son of Dath, King of Leinster[5]." The date of these *Dindsenchas* stories is unknown. There are however

---

[1] Printed by E. O'Curry in Appendix LXXXIX, p. 584 ff. of *Lectures on the MS. Materials of Ancient Irish History*.

[2] *Annals of Ulster*, s.a. 895 (=896).   [3] Transl. Stokes.

[4] Rennes, *Dindsenchas*, ed. and transl. Stokes, *Revue Celtique*, Vol. XVI, p. 63 f. A more detailed version from Y.B.L. is ed. and transl. by O'Curry, *Battle of Magh Lena*, p. 14 note. The text of the latter is printed by Windisch, *Irische Texte*, First Series, p. 112.

[5] *Revue Celtique*, Vol. XV, p. 311 ff.

indications that they are older than the version of the *Dindsenchas* in which they occur and which is itself believed to date from about 1200[1].

As regards the age of the saga Thurneysen[2] holds that it belongs to the same group as *Bricriu's Feast* and the earlier version of the *Sickbed of Cuchulainn*. These latter he believes to be earlier than the eleventh century[3]. We have seen that the story was known to Flannacán mac Cellaigh who died in 896, but it is not clear whether he knew it in written form or not. Like many other Irish sagas it may of course have been in circulation for centuries before it was committed to writing.

The persons with whom it is concerned figure in many other heroic sagas. It is still held by many scholars that these persons had their origin in myth—a view which used to be held in regard to the heroic stories of Greece and many other lands but which is now generally discredited. All that can be said with certainty is that if these persons had historical existence they must have lived long before the days of contemporary history. The genealogies and lists of kings indicate a period four or five centuries before the time of St Patrick—*i.e.* about the beginning of the Christian era—and this is the date to which Early Irish antiquarians assigned the reign of Conchobar.

The subject of the champion's portion is not confined to our saga. It forms the subject also, in a more expanded and elaborate form, of *Bricriu's Feast*. In the latter saga, however, several versions or stories appear to have been welded together, and the original theme to have been sophisticated by the introduction of the champion's wives. What is the relationship of our story to the stories which lie behind *Bricriu's Feast*? It would be interesting to know if oral tradition could transform a single story into versions so widely divergent as these[4]. We may observe that in the *Scél Mucci*, where so many Ulster heroes are introduced, Cuchulainn's name is never mentioned, whereas in *Bricriu's Feast* it is he who carries off the champion's portion. This would seem to suggest that our saga has come down to us in an early form. Moreover,

---

[1] See Thurneysen, *op. cit.* p. 499 and footnote 5 of p. 44 f.; cf. further, p. 71 below, s.v. *Blai briugu*.

[2] *Die Irische Helden- und Königsage*, p. 494.

[3] *Op. cit.* p. 415 f.   [4] Cf. note s.v. *is...fremaib*, ch. 18.

the hint in ch. 17 of Rawl. B. 512 suggests that a version of the story was current in which Cúrói mac Dári played a part. In *Bricriu's Feast* the Cúrói legend is introduced in much fuller form. Indeed, I am inclined to suspect that his (or Fergus') feat with the oak in the *Scél Mucci* contains an obscure and compressed hint of the decapitation test of valour in *Bricriu's Feast*. It is not easy otherwise to see why the incident is introduced.

There can be no doubt that the stories which form the subject of *Bricriu's Feast* and the *Scél Mucci* owe their origin to the same customs. Henderson, in his introduction to *Bricriu's Feast*[1], has collected instances from classical writers showing that the "championship in arms" was much coveted and the special "champion's portion" was an honoured custom among the ancient Gauls, as well as among other heroic peoples. Indeed, the picture of the feast in the Irish sagas corresponds closely to the picture presented by classical writers.

Thus we learn from Polybius[2] that large numbers of pigs were raised for food by the Gauls, and from Posidonius[3] that they ate much meat roasted, boiled or grilled, and little bread.

He further tells us: "Of old the flesh of the thighs which was set before them was taken by the strongest man. But if anyone else laid claim to it they came to blows and fought it out between themselves to the death."

According to Diodorus[4], "when they dine they all sit on the ground, not on chairs, and use the skins of wolves and dogs as mats....And beside them they have hearths with big fires and cauldrons and spits loaded with big joints of meat. They honour distinguished men with the best portions of the meat. They invite strangers to their feasts, and after dinner ask them who they are and what they desire. And when they are dining, some of the company often fall into an altercation and challenge one another and fight—they make nothing of death[5]." In the next chapter Diodorus tells us that when in the presence of their enemies "whenever anyone will listen to their challenges they

---

[1] Irish Texts Society, Vol. II, p. xi ff.   [2] XII, 4.
[3] Athenaeus IV, 36, 40.   [4] V, 28.
[5] For an account of the Gaulish feasts and general manner of living see Dottin, *Manuel pour servir à l'étude de l'Antiquité Celtique*[2] (Paris, 1915), p. 159 ff.

begin to glorify the valour of their forefathers and boast of their own prowess; and at the same time they deride and belittle their opponent and try by their speeches to rob him of all the courage he has in his heart."

It is probable that the series of ordeals by which the hero's right to the championship is vindicated in the *Scél Mucci* also had its origin in actual custom. The first ordeal, which occurs in ch. 7, consists of indiscriminate boasting, in which Munster families are well represented, though the Connaught champion, Cet mac Matach, outboasts them all. In the second ordeal (ch. 9 ff.) the Ulster champions in turn challenge Cet. He is able to vindicate his claim till the third ordeal—a duel of wit and words with Conall Cernach in which he is defeated. Finally in what I believe to be a fourth ordeal—that of missiles—Conall makes good his claim and divides the pig. And here it may not be out of place to call attention to Conall's remarkable prowess in eating—a prowess which is attributed to braves all over the world, and which reminds one of Thor's performance in the Norse poem *Thrymskviða*.

It may be added that the story of Mac Dathó's Pig is one incident in the long rivalry between Ulster and Connaught which culminated in the *Táin Bó Cúalnge*. It is one of the most finished specimens of the art of the ancient Irish story teller. The short account of Ailbe's travels at the end—a kind of *Dindsenchas*—which recalls the account of Twrch Trwyth in the story of Kilhwch and Olwen [1] (cf. ch. 20 and notes below) is perhaps a later addition to the original saga. Apart from this there is practically no antiquarian speculation in the saga, and supernatural and romantic elements are wholly absent. Women play hardly any part, and the humour is essentially such as would appeal to a male audience, as are also the details of the wounds inflicted by Cet on the seven Ulster heroes (ch. 9 ff.). It is a story about men for men, such as Dunnbó might have told to the heroes round the camp fire at the Battle of Allen [2].

---

[1] See Loth, *Les Mabinogion*[2], Paris, 1913; Lady Guest's transl. in *The Mabinogion* (published by Nutt, 1904), p. 126 ff.

[2] Ed. and transl. Stokes, *Revue Celtique*, Vol. xxiv, ch. 3, 7.

INCIPIT SCÉL MUCCI MIC DATHÓ

1. Boí rí amra for Laignib, .i. Mac Dathó a ainm. Bui cú oca. No-ditned in cu Lagniu uile. Ailbe ainm in chon, et lán hEriu dia aurdarcus. Tancas o Ailill ocus o Meidb do chungid in chon. I n-oen uair dano tancatar ocus techta Conchobair mic Nessa do chungid in chon chetna. Ro-ferad failte friu uile, et ructha chuci-sium isin ṁ-bruidin. Is í sein in t-ṡessed bruiden ro-boi i n-hErind in tan sin: .i. bruden Daderga i crích Cualand, et bruden Ḟorgaill Manaich, et bruden Mic Dareo i m-Brefni et bruden Dachoca i n-iarthor Mide et bruden Blai briuga i n-Ultaib. Secht ṅ-doruis isin bruidin ocus VII sligeda tréthi, et VII tellaige inti, et VII core, ocus dam ocus tinne in cach coire. In fer do-theiged iarsin t-ṡligi, do-bered in n-ael isin coire, et na tabrad don chét-gabail, issed no-ithed. Mani thucad ní don chét-tadall, ni bered a n-aill.

2. Ructha trá na techta 'na imdai chuci-sium do airiuc thuile dóib riasin feiss. Ro-raidset a n-athes[c]: "Do chungid in chon do-dechammar-ni ó Ailill ocus ó Meidb," ar tecta Connacht, "et dobertar tri fichit cét lilgach a chét-óir ocus carpat ocus da ech bas ferr la Connachta, ocus a chom-máin i cind bliadna cen-motha sin." "Dia chungid dano do-dechammar-ni," ar tecta Ulad, "o Chonchobar, ocus ni messo Conchobar do charait, ocus dano do thabairt sét ocus indile; ocus doberthar a chomméit cétna i cind bliadna et biaid deg-caratrad de."

3. Ro-lá din i socht mór intí Mac Dathó, cor-rabi tri thráth cen dig, cen biad, cen chotlod, acht co immorchor ón táib co araile. Is and ro-ráid a ben riss: "Is fota in troscud itái; atá biad lat cen co n-essara. Cid no-tái?" Ni tharat frecra for in mnaí, conid and ro-ráid in ben:

Tucad turbaid chotulta	do Mac Dathó co a thech,
ros-bói ní no-chomairled,	cen co labradar fri nech.
Asoí dosoi uaim fri fraig	in ferg fene co londgail,
a ben trebar dos-beir mod,	bith dia ceiliu cen chotlud.

In fer: Asbert Crimthand Nia[d] Nair,   ni thardda do rún do
     mnaib,
     run mna ní maith concelar,   main ar mug ni athenar.

In ben: Cid fri mnai atbertha-su,   mani thesbad ní aire?
     ní na téit do menma-su,   teiti menma neich aile.

In fer: Cu Mesroida Mic Dathó,   ba holc lathe etha dó,
     dofaeth mór fer find fria rath,   bid lia turim a chath.
     Manip do Chonchobar berthair,   is derb bid mogda
     in gním,
     no con faicebat a sluaig   bas mó do buaib na do thír.
     Mad do Ailill era   leis (*leg.* silis) falmag dar sin túaith,
     do-don-béra mac Matach,   ata-nebla i luim lúaith.

In ben: Tathut airle lim-sa ris   ní holc fri iarmairt ninni,
     tabair doib-sium diblínaib,   cumma cia thoetsat
     immi.

In fer: In chomairli doberi-siu   isí ním-déni cutal,
     Ailbe do-roid dia;   nicon fes cia o tucad.

4. Iarsin atracht suas ocus nom-bertaigedar. "Bad maith dún
tra," ol se, "ocus dona haigedaib dodn-ancatar." Anait side leis
trí laa ocus tri aidche, ocus gairmter chuci fo leith techta Connacht. "Ro-bá-sa tra," ar se, "i n-im-snim mor ocus cuntabairt
moir co ro-glé dam, .i. doratusa in coin do Ailill ocus do Meidb,
et tecat ar cend in chon co sochraid, ocus ros-bia lind ocus biad,
ocus bertait in coin, ocus is fochen dóib." Buidig techta Connacht
dond athesc.

Luid iarsin co tectaib Ulad. "Doratusa trá," ar se, "as mo
chuntabairt in coin do Chonchobar, et bid uallach tiastar ar a
chend .i. formná mathe Ulad. Bertait ascada, ocus ros-bia failte."
Budig techta Ulad.

5. I n-oen ló imorro ro-dalait-seom et anair ocus aniar. Ni
ro-follaiged leo-som dano. Táncatar dá cóiced hErend i n-oen ló,
co m-bátar i n-dorus bruidni Mic Dathó. Tic-seom féin immach
ocus dogní failte friu. "Ni ro-bar-fachlisem a ócu, ar apaide is
mo chen duib. Taít issin less." Lotar iarum uili isin m-bruidin.
Leth in tigi dano la Connachta ocus in leth aile la Ulto. Nir-
bo bec dano in tech: secht n-doruiss ind, ocus L imdad etir cech
da dorus. Niptar aigthe carat im fleid imorro bátar isin taig.

Sochaide díb ro-fuachtnaig fri araile. Tri chét bliadan ria ṅ-gein Christ ro-bói in cocad eturru. Marbthair dóib dano in mucc Mic Dathó. Tri fichit gamnach co a biathad saide co cend VII ṁ-bliadan. Tri neim imorro no-bíata[r], co ro-lathea ár fer ṅ-hErenn impi.

6. Tucad dóib iarum in mucc ocus XL dam dia tarsnu cenmotha in biad ar chena. Mac Dathó fessin icond ferdaigsecht. "Mo chen duib," ar se, "ni dabar samail riss sin. Ataat aige ocus mucca la Laigniu. A testa desin mairfider dúib imbárach." "Is maith in mucc," ar Conchobar. "Is maith imorro," ar Ailill. "Cinnas rainnfither in mucc, a Chonchobair?" ar Ailill. "Cinnas," ar Bricriu mac Carbaid anuas ane, "bale itaat láith gaile fer ṅ-hErend acht ar-raind ar galaib ocus ar chomramaib? Ocus dorat cách buille díb dar sróin a cheile riam." "Dentar," ar Ailill. "Is cóir," ar Conchobar. "Atát gillai dún istaig ro-im-thigitar in cocrích."

7. "Ricfaiter a les do gillai innocht, a Chonchobair," ar Senlaech Arad al-luachraib Conalad aníar. "Ba menic ag méth díb d'facbail acum-sa ocus rota Luachra Dedad fó tóin." "Ba méthiu an ag foracbaisiu ocain-ni, .i. do brathair fadéin .i. Cruachniu mac Rúadluim a Cruachnaib Conalad." "Nir-bo ferr saide," ar Lugaid mac Conrúi, "andás in Loth mór mac Fergusa maic Leti foracbad la Echbél mac Dedad i Temair Lochra." "Cinnas fir lib," ol Celtchair mac Uthechair, "Conganchness mac Dedad do marbad dam-sa ocus a chend do beim de."

8. Immo-tarla trá dóib fo deoid co tarat in t-oinfer for firu hErend .i. Cet mac Matach. Do-fúargaib side imorro fair a gasced uas gaiscedaib in t-sluaig et ro-gab scín inna láim ocus dessid ocon muicc. "Fagabar tra," ar se, "do feraib hErend tairismi comrama frim-sa no lécud nam-mucci do raind dam."

9. Ros-lá i socht na h-Ulto. "Atchí, a Loegaire," or Conchobar. "Ni ba fír," ar Loegaire, "Cét do raind na mucce ar ar m-belaib-ni." "An bic, a Loegaire, co rot-acilliur," ar Cet. "Is bés dúib-si in far n-Ultaib," ar Cet, "cech mac gaibes gaisced acaib is cucain-ni cend a báire. Dochua[i]daisiu dano isin cocrích. Imma-tarraid dún inti; foracbais in roth ocus in carpat ocus na heocho. Atrullais fein ocus gai triut. Nis-toirchi in muicc fón innasin." Dessid side dano.

10. "Ni ba fír," or laech find mór do-dechaid assind imdai,
"Cet do raind na mucci ar ar m-bélaib-ni." "Coich andso?" or
Cet. "Is ferr do laech andaisiu," or cach, "Oengus mac Lama
Gabaid sin do Ultaib." "Cid diata Lám Gábuid for th'athair-siu?"
or Cet. "Cid ám?" "Ro-fetar-sa," or Cet. "Dochuadusa sair fecht
and. Eigther immum; do-roich cách, do-roich dano Lám. Tarlaic
urchor do gai mór dam-sa. Dos-leicim-se dano do-som in ṅ-gai
cétna, co m-ben a laim de, co m-bui for lár. Cid dobérad a mac
do chomram frim-sa?" Téit Oengus ina suide.

11. "In comram do thairisem beus," or Cet, "no in mucc do
raind dam-sa." "Ni ba fír ar-raind duit-siu chetumus," ar laech
find mór de Ultaib. "Cia andso?" or Cet. "Eogan mac Durthacht
sin," ar cách, [.i. rí Fernmaigi]. "Atchonnarc-sa riam," or Cet.
"Cia airm i n-domḟacca?" ar Eogan. "I n-dorus do thaige oc
tabairt tana bó uait. Ro-héged immum-sa isin tír. Tanacaisiu
fon égim. Ro-thelgis gai ḟorm-sa corra-ba as mo scíath. Dollecim-
se duit-siu in ṅ-gai cétna, colluid trét chend, ocus co m-bert do
ṡúil as do chind." Atotchiat fir hErenn co n-oén ṡúil. Messe tall
in t-ṡúil aile as do chind." Dessid side dano.

12. "Frithalid dano, a Ulto, in comram beus!" ar Cet. "Nis-
raindfe innossa," ar Munremor mac Gergind. "Inné seo Munremur?" ar Cet. "Is me ro-glan mo gó fo deóid a Munremur," or Cet.
"Ní ḟuilet trí thráth and o thucusa tri láich-cind uait im chend
do chétmic as t' ḟerund." Dessid side dano.

"In comram beus!" or Cet. "Rot-bia són," ar Mend mac Sal-
cholcan. "Cia so?" or Cet. "Mend," or cách. "Cid ane," or Cet,
"mac na m-bachlach cusna les-anmannaib do chomram chucum;
ar ba úaim-se fúair th'athair in t-ainm sin, .i. messe ra-ben a ṡail
de do chlaidiub, conna ruc acht oen-choís úaim. Cid dobérad mac
ind oen-choisseda chucum?" Dessid side dano.

13. "In comram beus!" or Cet. "Rot-bia," or laech líath mór
forgránna do Ultaib. "Cia so?" or Cet. "Celtchair mac Cuthechair
sin," or cách. "An bic, a Cheltchair," or Cet, "manip dom thuar-
cain fo chetóir. Ro-tanac-sa, a Cheltchair, co dorus do thigi. Foheged immum. Tánic cách. Tanacaisiu dano. Dot-luid i m-bernai ar
mo chind-sa. Do-reilgis gae dam-sa. Ro-thelgiusa gai n-aill chu-

cutsu, co n-dechaid triat [ṡ]liasait ocus tria uachtur do macraille. Atái co ṅ-galur fúail ond uair sin, no co rucad mac no ingen duit ond uair sin. Cid dot-bérad chucum-sa?" Dessid side dano.

14. "In comram beus!" or Cet. "Rot-bia son," or Cúscraid Mend Macha, mac Conchobair. "Cuich seo?" ar Cet. "Cuscraid," or cách, "is adbar ríg ar deilb." "Ni buide frit," or in gilla. "Maith," or Cet. "Cucainn cetna thanacais do chét-gasciud, a gillai. Immatarraid dún issin chocrich. Foracbais trian do muntire, ocus is amlaid dochuadais ocus gai triat bragit, conna hetai focul fort chend i córai, ar ro-loitt in gái féthi do braget, conid Cúscraid Mend atot-chomnaic ond uair sin." Dorat tra fon n-innasin ail forsin cóiced uile.

15. In tan *din* rom-bertaigestar oc on muicc ocus scían inna láim, co n-accatar Conall Cernach istech. Is and tarblaiṅg for lár in taige. Ferait Ulaid imorro failte móir fri Conall. Is and ro-lá Conchobar in cennide dia chind ocus *n*od-mbertaigedar. "Is maith lind ar cuit do thairiuc," ar Conall. "Cia rannas dúib?" "Rod-dét dond fir nod-ranna," ar Conchobar, ".i. Cet mac Matach." "In fir a Chit," ar Conall, "tusso do raind nam-muicce?" Is and asbert Cet:

R.   "Fochen Conall!   cride licce,
       londbruth loga,   luchair ega,
       gusfland ferge!   fo chích curad
       crechtaig cathbuadaig adcomsa mac Findchoeme frim."

Conid and atbert Conall:

R.   "Fochen Cet,
       Cet mac Matach!   magen curad,
       cride n-ega,   eithre n-ela,
       eirr trén tressa,   trethan ágach,
       cain tarb tnúthach.   Cet mac Magach!
       "Bid mend inar n-im-chomruic-ni ón," ar Conall,
       "ocus bid mend inar n-im-scarad,
       bid airscela la Fer ṁ-brot,
       bid fiadnaisi la Fer manath.
       Adcichset airg loman londgliaid,
       fer dar fer is taig seo innocht.

16. "Eirg ón muicc *din!*" or Conall. " Cid dano dot-bérad-su chucci?" ar Cett. "Is fir," or Conall, "do chungid chomraime chucum-sa. Dobér oen-chomram duit, a Cheit," ar Conall. "Toṅgu na toṅgat mo thuath, o ra-gabus gai im láim, nach menic robá cen chend Connachtaig fóm chind oc cotlud, ocus cen guin duine cech oen lá ocus cech oen aidchi." "Is fir," or Cet, "at ferr do laéch andó-sa. Mad Anluan no-beth is taig, doberad comram ar araile duit. Is anim dún na fil is taig." "Atá imorro," ar Conall ic tabairt chind Ánlúain assa chriss, ocus nos-leice do Chet ar a bruinni, cor-roimid a loim fola for a beolu. Ro-gab side imorro ón muic, et dessid Conall aicce.

17. "Tecat don chomram a fecht-sa!" ar Conall. Ní fríth ón la Connachta laech a thairismi. Doratad imorro damdabach dona boccótib immi imm[a] cuairt, ar ro-boi droch-costud istaig do chloendiburgun la droch-daine. Luid iarum Conall do raind nam-mucci ocus gebid dano cend in tarra ina beolo, cor-ránic dó raind nam-mucci. Ra[suig] in tairr .i. aere ind nónbair, connafargaib ní de.

18. Ni thara[t] imorro do Chonnachtaib acht a da cois nam-mucci fo brágid. Ba bec dano la Connachta a cuit. Atragat saide; atragat dano Ulaid, cor-riacht cách araile. Ro-bói tra builli dar ó i suidiu, co m-ba comard ra sliss in taige in carnail *r*o-bái for lár in taigi, co m-batar na srotha don chrú forsna dorsi. Maidit dano na sluaig for na dorsi, cor-ralsat grith mór co suifed fuil mol for lár ind liss, .i. cach oc truastad a cheile. Is and gabais Fergus dóib dair mór ro-bói for lár ind liss assa fremaib. Maidit immach dano as ind liss. Doberar in cath i n-dorus ind liss.

19. Is and luid Mac Dathó immach ocus in cú inna láim, co ro-leiced eturro, dús cia díb no-thogad, .i. rús con. Do-ráiga in cú Ulto, ocus ro-leci for ár Connacht, ar ro-mebaid for Connachta. Asberat-som, iss im-maigib Ailbe ro-gab in cú fertais in charpait fo Ailill ocus fo Meidb. Is and donáraill Ferloga ara Aililla ocus Medba, .i. cor-rala a cholaind for leth, ocus co ro-an a chend i fertais in charpait. Atbert dano, is de atá Mag Ailbe, .i. Ailbe ainm in chon.

20. Dolluid am-maidm andes for Beluch Mugna se*ch* Róirind for Áth Midbine i m-Mastin, sech Druim Criaig, fris rater Cell

Dara indiu, sech Ráith Imgain i Fid ṅ-Gaible, do Áth mac Lugnai, sech Druim Da Maige, for Drochet Cairpre. Oc Áth Chind
Chon i m-Biliu is and ro-lá cend in chon asin charput. Ic techt
iar fraechrud Mide síar is and donarlaic Ferloga isin fraech, .i. ara
Alilla, ocus ro-liṅg isin carput iar cúl Chonchobair, cor-ra-gaib
a chend dar aiss. "Beir buide n-anacuil a Chonchobair!" ar se.
"T'óg-ríar," ar Conchobar. "Ní ba mór," ar Ferloga, ".i. mo breith
latt do Emain Macha, ocus mná oentama Ulad ocus a n-ingena
macdacht do gabail cepoce cech nóna immum, co n-erbrat:
"Ferloga mo lennan-sa." Ba écen ón, ar ní laimtis chena la Conchobar, et ra-leiced Ferloga dar Ath Luain síar dia bliadna ocus
da gabair Chonchobair leis co n-allaib óir friu.

THE STORY OF MAC DATHÓ'S PIG

1. There was a famous king of Leinster. Mac Dathó was his name. He had a hound; the hound defended the whole of Leinster. The hound's name was Ailbe, and Ireland was full of its fame. Messengers came from Ailill and Medb asking for the hound. Moreover at the same time there came also messengers from Conchobar Mac Nessa to ask for the same hound. They were all made welcome and brought to him in the hall. That is one of the six halls that were in Ireland at that time, the others being the hall of Da Derga in the territory of Cualu, and the hall of Forgall Manach, and the hall of Mac Dareo in Brefne, and the hall of Da Choca in the west of Meath, and the hall of Blai the landowner in Ulster. There were seven doors in that hall, and seven passages through it, and seven hearths in it, and seven cauldrons, and an ox and a salted pig in each cauldron. Every man who came along the passage used to thrust the flesh-fork into a cauldron, and whatever he brought out at the first catch was his portion. If he did not obtain anything at the first attempt he did not have another.

2. Now the messengers were brought to him in his place that he might learn their requests before the feast. They delivered their message: "We have come from Ailill and from Medb to beg the hound," said the messengers of Connaught; "and there shall be given three score hundred milch cows at once, and a chariot and two horses, the best in Connaught, and their equivalent gifts at the end of a year in addition to this."

"We also have come from Conchobar to ask for it," said the messengers from Ulster; "—and Conchobar's value as a friend is no less—and to give you treasure and cattle; and the same amount shall be given you at the end of a year, and close friendship will be the result."

3. Thereupon our Mac Dathó lapsed into total silence and in this way he was a whole day (?) without drink, without food, without sleep, tossing from side to side. Then his wife said to him: "You are making a long fast. There is food beside you but you don't eat it. What ails you?"

He gave the woman no answer, so the woman said:

"Sleeplessness fell upon Mac Dathó at his home. There was something upon which he was brooding without speaking to anyone.

"He turns away from me and turns to the wall, the warrior of the Fían (?) of fierce valour; it causes concern to his prudent wife that her husband is sleepless."

The Man: "Crimthann Nia Nair said: 'Do not tell your secret to women.' The secret of a woman is not well kept. A treasure is not entrusted to a slave."

The Woman: "Even to a woman you should speak if nothing should be lost thereby. A thing which your own mind cannot penetrate the mind of another will penetrate."

The Man: "The hound of Mesroeda Mac Dathó, evil was the day when they sent for it. Many tall and fair-haired men will fall on account of it. The strife about it will be more than we can reckon.

"Unless it is given to Conchobar it will certainly be a churl's act. His hosts will not leave behind them anything more of cattle than of land.

"If it be refused to Ailill (?), he will hew down a heap of corpses (?) across the country. Mac Matach will carry us off, he will crush us into bare ashes."

The Woman: "I have advice for you about it. I am not bad at directing an affair. Give it to them both. It is all the same whoever perishes for it."

The Man: "The counsel you offer is helpful to me. Ailbe.... It is not known by whom it was brought."

4. After that he arose and made a flourish. "Let us then," said he, "and the guests who have come to us be well entertained." They remain with him three days and three nights, and the messengers of Connaught were summoned to him in private: "Now I have been in great perplexity and doubt," said he, "until it became clear to me that I should give the hound to Ailill and Medb; and let them come for the hound formally, and they shall

have drink and food, and shall take the hound and welcome." The messengers of Connaught were pleased with the intimation.

He then went to the messengers from Ulster: "I have ceased to have any hesitation," said he, "in giving the hound to Conchobar, and let him and the host of Ulster nobles come for it proudly. They shall receive presents and they will be welcome." The messengers from Ulster were pleased.

5. Now the people from East and West made their tryst for the same day. Moreover they did not neglect it. On the same day the two provinces of Ireland made their journey until they reached the door of Mac Dathó's hall. He went out himself and welcomed them: "O heroes, we did not expect you. However you are welcome. Come into the enclosure." Then they all went into the hall, and half the house was occupied by the Connaughtmen, and the other half by the Ulstermen. Now the house was not a small one. There were seven doors in it, and fifty places between each pair of doors. They were not however the faces of friends at a feast which were in that house. One party was at feud with the other. There had been warfare between them for three hundred years before the birth of Christ.

Now Mac Dathó's pig was slaughtered for them. For seven years sixty milch cows supplied its food. On poison however it had been nourished and the massacre of the men of Erin took place through it.

6. Now the pig was brought to them, and forty oxen as a relish, and other food as well. Mac Dathó himself was acting as steward. "Welcome to you," said he; "the equal to this cannot be found. Bullocks and pigs are not lacking in Leinster. Whatever is lacking now will be slaughtered for you tomorrow."

"The pig is good," said Conchobar.

"It is indeed good," said Ailill. "How shall the pig be divided, Conchobar?"

"How," said Bricriu mac Carbaid...from above, "in the place wherein are the brave heroes of the men of Ireland, except by dividing according to brave deeds and trophies? And each of you has hit another over the nose before now."

"Let it be done," said Ailill.

"Very proper," said Conchobar. "We have heroes present who have raided the borderland."

7. "You will have need of your young men tonight, O Conchobar," said Senlaech Arad from Conalad Luachra in the West. "You have often left a fat bullock of your number lying dead on his back on the Luachra Dedad roads."

"It was a fatter bullock that you left behind with us, namely your own brother, Cruachniu mac Rúadluim from Cruachan Conalad."

"He was no better," said Lugaid mac Cúrói, "than the great Loth the son of Fergus mac Léti, who was left dead by Echbél mac Dedad in Tara Luachra."

"What do you think of this," said Celtchair mac Uthechair, "—my having killed Conganchness mac Dedad and cut off his head?!"

8. However it so fell out among them in the end that a single champion, Cet mac Matach, got supremacy over the men of Ireland. Moreover he flaunted his valour on high above the valour of the host, and took a knife in his hand and sat down beside the pig.

"Let someone be found now among the men of Ireland," said he, "to endure battle with me, or leave the pig to me to divide!"

9. Silence fell upon the men of Ulster.

"You see that, Loegaire!" said Conchobar.

"It is intolerable," said Loegaire, "for Cet to divide up the pig before our faces."

"Stop a bit, Loegaire, that I may speak to you," said Cet. "You have a custom among you in Ulster," said Cet, "that every youth among you on receiving arms makes us his objective. Now you came into the borderland, and we encountered there. You left behind the wheel and the chariot and the horses. You yourself made off with a spear through you. You will not get the pig in that way."

Thereupon the other sat down.

10. "It is intolerable," said a tall fair hero who had risen from his place, "that Cet should divide the pig before our faces."

"Whom have we here?" asked Cet.

"He is a better hero than you are," said everyone; "he is Oengus mac Láma Gábuid of Ulster."

"Why is your father called Lám Gábuid?" asked Cet.

"Well why?"

"I know," said Cet. "I once went eastward. The alarm was raised around me. Everyone came on and Lám came too. He threw a cast of his great spear at me. I sent the same spear back to him, and it struck off his hand, so that it lay on the ground. What could bring his son to give me combat?"

Oengus sat down.

11. "Keep up the contest further," said Cet, "or else let me divide the pig."

"It is intolerable that you should take precedence in dividing the pig," said a tall fair hero of Ulster.

"Whom have we here?" asked Cet.

"That is Eogan mac Durthacht," said everyone. [He is king of Fernmag.]

"I have seen him before," said Cet.

"Where have you seen me?" asked Eogan.

"At the door of your house, when I deprived you of a drove of cattle. The alarm was raised around me in the country-side. You came at that cry. You cast a spear at me so that it stuck out of my shield. I cast the spear back at you so that it pierced your head and put out your eye. It is patent to the men of Ireland that you are one-eyed. It was I who struck out the other eye from your head."

Thereupon the other sat down.

12. "Prepare now, men of Ulster, for further contest," said Cet.

"You will not divide it yet," said Munremor mac Gergind.

"Is not that Munremor?" asked Cet. "I am the man who last cleaned my spears in Munremor," said Cet. "It is not yet a whole day(?) since I took three heads of heroes from you out of your land, and among them the head of your eldest son."

Thereupon the other sat down.

"Further contest!" said Cet.

"That you shall have," said Mend mac Sálcholcán.

"Who is this?" asked Cet.

"Mend," said everyone.

"What next!" said Cet, "sons of rustics with nick-names to contest with me!—for it was from me your father got that name. It was I who struck off his heel with my sword, so that he took away only one foot when he left me. What could encourage the son of the one-footed man to fight with me?"

Thereupon the other sat down.

13. "Further contest!" said Cet.

"That you shall have," said a grey, tall, very terrible hero of Ulster.

"Who is this?" asked Cet.

"That is Celtchair mac Uthechair," said everyone.

"Stop a bit, Celtchair!" said Cet, "unless we are to come to blows at once. I came, Celtchair, to the door of your house. The alarm was raised around me. Everyone came up. You came too. You went into the doorway in front of me. You cast a spear at me. I cast another spear at you so that it pierced your thigh and the upper part of the fork of your legs. You have had a ... disease ever since. Since then neither son nor daughter has been begotten by you. What could encourage you to fight with me?"

Thereupon the other sat down.

14. "Further contest!" said Cet.

"That you shall have," said Cúscraid Mend Macha, the son of Conchobar.

"Who is this?" asked Cet.

"Cúscraid," said the others. "He has the makings of a king to judge from his appearance."

"No thanks to you," said the boy.

"Well," said Cet, "it was to us you came in the first place, boy, for your first trial of arms. There was an encounter between us in that borderland. You left a third of your people behind; and it is thus you went, with a spear through your throat, so that you have not an articulate word in your head; for the spear has injured the tendons of your throat, and that is why you have been nick-named Cúscraid the Stammerer ever since."

And in this manner he flouted the whole province.

15. Now while he was making flourishes about the pig
with a knife in his hand they saw Conall Cernach entering. He
bounded into the centre of the house. The men of Ulster gave a
great welcome to Conall. Then Conchobar whipped the hood from
his head and made a flourish.

"I am glad that my portion is in readiness," said Conall.
"Who is he who is making the division for you?"

"It has been granted to the man who is dividing it," said
Conchobar, "namely Cet mac Matach."

"Is it right, Cet," asked Conall, "that you should divide the pig?"
Then Cet answered:

"Welcome, Conall! Heart of stone,
Fierce glowing mass of fire, brightness of ice,
Red strength of wrath! Under the breast of the hero
Who deals wounds, and is victorious in battle
I see the son of Findchoem before me."

Whereupon Cet replied:

"Welcome, Cet,
Cet Mac Matach! great (?) hero,
Heart of ice....
Strong chariot-hero of battle, battling sea,
Beautiful fierce bull, Cet mac Magach!
"It will be clear in our encounter," said Conall,
    "and it will be clear in our separation.
There will be a fine saga in Fer m-brot (?)
There will be ill tidings in Fer manath (?)
The heroes will see a lion (?) fierce in battle,
There will be a rough onset
    in this house to-night."

16. "Get up from the pig now," said Conall.
"But what should bring you to it?" asked Cet.

"It is quite proper," said Conall, "that you should challenge
me! I accept your challenge to single combat, Cet," said Conall.
"I swear what my tribe swears, that since I took a spear in my
hand I have not often slept without the head of a Connaughtman under my head, and without having wounded a man every
single day and every single night."

"It is true," said Cet. "You are a better hero than I am. If

Anlúan were in the house he would offer you yet another contest. It is a pity for us that he is not in the house."

"He is though," said Conall, taking the head of Anlúan from his belt, and throwing it at Cet's breast with such force that a gush of blood burst over his lips. Cet then left the pig, and Conall sat down beside it.

17. "Let them come to the contest now!" said Conall. There was not found among the men of Connaught a hero to keep it up. They made however a wall of shields in a circle around him, for the bad practice had begun among those bad men there of evil casting. Conall then went to divide the pig, and takes the tail-end in his mouth and so attained to a division of the pig. He devoured the hind-quarters—a load for nine men—until he had left nothing of it.

18. Moreover he did not give to the men of Connaught anything except the two fore-quarters of the pig. Now the men of Connaught thought their portion was small. They sprang up, and the men of Ulster sprang up, and then they came to close quarters. Then it came to blows over the ears there until the heap on the floor of the house was as high as the wall of the house, and there were streams of blood running through the doors. Then the hosts broke through the doors so that a great uproar arose, until the blood on the ground of the liss would have turned a millshaft, everyone striking his fellow. Then Fergus seized by the roots a great oak which was growing in the midst of the liss and wielded it against them. Thereupon they break forth out of the liss. A combat takes place at the entrance of the liss.

19. Then Mac Dathó went forth leading the hound, and the hound was let loose among them to find out which of them its instinct would choose. The hound chose the men of Ulster and he set it to slaughtering the men of Connaught—for the men of Connaught had been routed. They say it is in the plains of Ailbe that the hound seized the pole of the chariot in which Ailill and Medb were. There Ferloga, the charioteer of Ailill and Medb, ran it down, striking its body aside, while its head remained on the pole of the chariot. They say moreover that Mag Ailbe is so named from this incident, for Ailbe was the hound's name.

20. Their flight turned southwards, over Bellaghmoon, past Reerin, over Áth Midbine in Mastiu, past Drum Criach which to-day is called Kildare, past Rathangan into Feighcullen to the Ford of Mac Lugna, past the hill of the two plains over Cairpre's Bridge. At the Ford of the Dog's Head in Farbill the dog's head fell from the chariot. Coming westwards over the heath of Meath, Ferloga, Ailill's charioteer, lay down in the heather and sprang into the chariot behind the back of Conchobar, and in this way seized his head from behind. "Buy your freedom, Conchobar," said he. "Make your own terms," said Conchobar. "It will not be much," replied Ferloga, "namely, you to take me with you to Emain Macha, and the women of Ulster and their young daughters to sing a panegyric to me every evening saying: 'Ferloga is my darling.'" There was no help for it, for they did not dare do otherwise for fear of Conchobar; and that day a year hence Ferloga was sent across Athlone westwards, and a pair of Conchobar's horses with him, with golden bridles.

THE STORY OF MAC DATHÓ'S PIG

NOTES

1. *rí amra*. Harl. 5280 has *rí brug* (? for *bruiden*) *amre*, i.e. presumably a 'royal hall,' but this does not make very good sense with what follows. Probably *brug* is the contracted form of *brugaid*, 'hospitaller,' 'landowner.' Rawl. B. 512 has *Bái brughaid amra*. The correct reading is perhaps *rig-brugaid amra*. Cf. *flaith-brugaid* (Meyer, *Contributions*, s.v. *brugaid*).

for Laignib, lit. 'over the men of Leinster.' The 'pl. noun (cf. Index s.v. *Ulaid*) suggests that the local units were tribal rather than territorial, i.e. a district is thought of in terms of the (pl.) name of the people who occupy it, as in most ancient languages. For *for* Harl. 5280 has *la*, i.e. 'The men of Leinster had,' etc.

.i., for *idon*, usual Ir. scribal abbrev., 'that is,' 'viz.' for L. *id est*; in Irish MSS. commonly written *.i.* Cf. Dottin, 'Sur l'emploi de *.i.*,' in *Miscellany presented to Kuno Meyer* (Halle, 1912), p. 102 f.

Buí...uile, lit. 'There was a hound at him. The hound used to defend all Leinster.' For *no-ditned* Harl. 5280 has *no imtigid*. Cf. vocab. s.v. *imm-thigim*; Rawl. B. 512 *no imthig[ed] Laig[niu] uili a n-oenló*, 'He had a hound that would run round all Leinster in one day' (Meyer). H. 3. 18, *no imdichedh*, 'used to defend' (*imb-dífich*), is no doubt the original. The form of Rawl. was understood as *imtéiged*, *imtheiged*, 'used to go about,' and *a n-oen ló* added to make sense. LL. replaced *imdiched* by a more familiar word *no-ditned*. *No-ditned*, *no* is here the untranslatable preverbal particle used with the secondary present in an imperfect sense.

Ailbe...aurdarcus. Note the (regular) omission of the verb 'to be.'

Tancas...chon, lit. 'There came from Ailill and from Medb to demand the hound.' Harl. 5280 *Dotoet techta*, Rawl. B. 512 *Dotiaghat...techta* 'messengers came.'

do chungid etc. Note the (regular) aspiration of the initial consonant after *do* and after *in* (gen. masc. of the article). Note also the gen. after the verbal noun.

I n-oen uair. Probably *i n-* represents the article. Cf. *in tan sin* below. Note that the final *n* of *i n-* is prefixed to a following vowel. Harl. 5280 and Rawl. B. 512 have *immalle* (*imorro* R.) *de dechotar ocus techta ulad* (⁊ *Conchobair* R.).

in chon chetna. Note the (regular) aspiration of the adj. after the gen. sing. of the masc. noun.

ro...uile, lit. 'welcome was given to them all.'

chuci-sium, i.e. to Mac Dathó.

isin m-bruidin. *Isin*, prep. *i* combined with the article. Cf. O'Connell, *Old Irish Grammar*, § 43. Note the nasalisation after the acc. The exact meaning of the word *bruden* is uncertain. The fullest description is to be found in *Bricriu's Feast* (transl. Henderson, Irish Texts Society) and in *The Destruction of Da Derga's Hostel*. Their construction appears to be of the frailest materials, and is in curious contrast with what appears to be, in some cases, a permanent institution. No doubt wood and even more perishable material, such as mud and wattle (cf. *Bricriu's Feast*, ch. 25 f.), were the chief building materials in use in ancient Ireland except for ecclesiastical purposes. The passage in *Da Derga's Hostel*, ch. 31, seems to suggest that these halls were erected at four cross-roads, and that they were used as asylums or halls of refuge where fugitives who had aroused a blood-feud might take refuge. Cf. *The Destruction of Da Choca's Hostel*, ch. 31, and the poem published by Stokes (with translation) as an appendix (*Revue Celtique*, vol. XXI, pp. 315, 396 f.). It will be observed that in this poem as well as in the other lists cited by Stokes in his note on p. 396 some of the names and details of the keepers of the *bruidne* differ from those in our text. Cf. introduction, p. 5 above. It would seem on the whole that the hostels were used as scenes of festivity and refreshment primarily in the Irish sagas, though it is very probable that they came to be used for this purpose originally as being sacrosanct, and safe places in which to lay aside, or 'hang up' arms (cf. note below, s.v. *do-fúargaib*).

Is...boi, lit. 'It is that (which is) one of the six halls (which) was,' etc. For *sessed* Windisch read *seised*, but *s* appears to be fairly clear in LL.; cf. Harl. 5280 *sesed*. Rawl. B. 512 has *coíced*.

in tan sin, used adverbially, 'at that time.' *In* is the article.

.i. Cf. note on *.i.* above.

i n-iarthor Mide, i.e. in the west of the ancient kingdom of Meath, in modern Westmeath.

briuga (gen.), 'landowner,' 'hospitaller' (Meyer); 'landwirth,' 'pächter' (Windisch); 'landholder' (Leahy). It would be interesting to know more about the keepers of these *bruidne*. Mac Dathó himself belonged to the royal family of Leinster, his brother being Mesgegra (cf. Index). Bricriu is generally to be found in Conchobar's suite. Om. *et...n-Ultaib* Rawl.

i n-Ultaib. Harl. 5280 reads *a coic. Concob.*

Secht ṅ-. Note the nasalisation (regular) after *secht*. For the description of the hall cf. *The Destruction of Da Derga's Hostel* (transl. Stokes, *Revue Celtique*, vol. XXII, p. 36), where also there are seven doorways and seven 'bedrooms' (so Stokes) between every two doorways. In the poem on the hostels of Ireland to which ref. has been made above (cf. p. 5) only four doors are mentioned. For a general description of an old Irish interior see Dottin, *Manuel de l'Antiquité celtique*[2] (Paris, 1915), p. 154.

VII *sligeda tréthi*. *Slige*, lit. 'a cutting,' hence 'a road.' The passage perhaps means that seven roads led to the house.

core. Cf. refs. s.v. *Secht ṅ-* above.

dam ocus tinne. From Polybius (XII. 4) we learn that the ancient Celts had large numbers of pigs for food; and Poseidonius tells us (Athenaeus IV. 36) that the Gauls ate much meat roast, boiled and grilled, and little bread. Cf. Dottin, *Manuel de l'Antiquité celtique*[2], p. 161.

In...theiged, Ir. idiom for the indefinite subject, lit. 'the man who used to come,' i.e. 'every man who came.'

iarsin t-sligi, 'kam des Weges' (Thurneysen); 'came along the road (Meyer); 'after a journey' (Leahy); Strachan translates *iar* 'along'; Windisch (here) 'nach,' 'räumlich.' Note the (regular) aspiration after the dat. sing. of the article *-sint* (dat. after *iar*) and the change of the original *d* of the article to *t* before the aspirated *s* (pronounced *h*). For the custom among the ancient Gauls of insisting on travellers partaking of their hospitality, see Athenaeus IV. 34; Dottin, *Manuel de l'Antiquité celtique*[2] (Paris, 1915), p. 165.

na tabrad, 'what he would bring forth.' H. 3. 18 has *a taibredh* for E.Ir. *a ndobered. Na* represents doubling of *a-n (ana(n))* which becomes *na.* Cf. Pedersen, *Vergleichende Grammatik der keltischen Sprachen,* vol. II, sec. 541 (3).

issed no-ithed, lit. '(It) is it (that) he used to eat.' The relative is omitted. *don (do+in).* Cf. vocab. s.v. *do,* probably here confused with *di* q.v.

chét-, note the (regular) aspiration after the dat. sing. of the article.

Mani...tadall, lit. 'If he should draw nothing at the first attempt.' Harl. 5280 reads *mani thucad vero ni don ced gabail ni bēd araild.* Rawl. B. 512 7 *mine tuctha sénni anis don cétgab[áil], ni bíd araill dó,* 'and if nothing were brought up at the first thrust, there was no other for him' (Meyer).

don. See vocab. s.v. *di,* and cf. above.

a n-aill. Note the (regular) retention of the nasal before the initial vowel after the acc. sing. neut. of the article.

2. *'na imdai.* So Meyer, no doubt correctly (cf. chs. 5, 10 below). Rawl. B. 512 has *isin lebaid,* 'in his bed' (Meyer). H. 3. 18 has *ina iomdaigh,* and Harl. 5280 *ina imga* (for *imda*), which confirms Meyer's reading. Windisch read *naimdai* which is certainly erroneous. Leahy translates, 'As he sat upon his throne'; Duvau, 'dans la chambre' (following Stokes, see vocab. below); Thurneysen, 'auf seiner Pritsche'; Dottin, 'chambre,' 'lit.'

do...dóib, 'to be asked their pleasure' (Meyer); 'dass er ihr Begehr vernehme' (Thurneysen); 'that he might learn of their requests' (Leahy). *Airec* is not a common verb. Windisch suggests that it is probably identical with *airec,* infin. of *air-ecar,* 'invenitur.' Cf. his Gloss. s.v.

feiss. Leahy transl. 'before they had their meal'; Duvau understood this as a reference to the great feast at Tara (cf. Keating, Ir. Texts Soc., vol. II, pp. 133, 251), which seems to me very improbable. Rawl. B. 512 has *riassa dobertha a cuitig dóib,* 'before their ration was brought to them' (Meyer); Harl. 5280 has *riesiuu dob[er]ta ambíad andocom;* H. 3. 18 *riasíu diberthae a mbiad doib,* 'Before their victuals were brought to them.' *Feiss* is here probably the ordinary supper from the cauldrons prepared for the new arrivals after their journey, cf. ch. 1. For a description of the feasts of the ancient Celts, as well as references to classical authorities, see Dottin, *Manuel de l'Antiquité celtique*[2] (Paris, 1915), p. 164 ff. Among the most interesting of the latter we may cf. Diodorus Siculus, V, 28; Athenaeus,

IV, 40. *Feiss, fess* is the verbal noun of *foaid*, 'he spends the night,' which by extension came to mean 'feasting,' 'feast.'

n-athes[c], so Windisch, on the authority of H. 3. 18 (*aithescae*) and Harl. 5280 (*athiusca*). Rawl. B. 512 has *aithesca*, LL. has *athes*. Note the (regular) nasalisation of the initial vowel after the 3rd pl. of the possess. adj.

do-dechammar-ni, lit. 'came we.'

Connacht. Harl. 5280 adds *i. o Medb 7 o Ailill.*

a chét-óir (*chét* + *óir*), 'the first hour,' 'at once.' Cf. adverbial phrases like *in tan sin.* H. 3. 18 *hi cetoir*; Harl. 5280 om.

ferr, compar. used for superl. Note the (regular) aspiration of the initial consonant after the relative form of the copula. Harl. 5280 has *dech*, the Old Irish superl. So also H. 3. 18.

a chom-máin. The aspiration shows *a* to be 3rd sing. m. (n.) '(the) equivalent of it,' i.e. of the gift.

bliadna, gen. sing. of *bliadain*. So edd. LL. has only the contracted form *bl.*; Rawl. B. 512, *bli.*

la Connachta. Harl. 5280 reads *la connša fo c. uair 7 a comain.*

Dia chungid, di + *a*, *do* appearing as *di* when combined with the poss. pron. Note the (regular) aspiration of the initial consonant of *cungid* after the 3rd sing. masc. of the possess. pron.; lit. 'To his asking,' i.e. 'for asking him.'

Ulad, gen. of *Ulaid*, 'The men of Ulster.'

ni...charait, lit. 'Not worse (is) Conchobar for a friend,' i.e. than Ailill and Medb. Thurneysen transl. 'C. ist als Freund nicht weniger wert'; K. Meyer, 'C. is no worse friend (than A. and M.)." Note the aspiration (regular) after *do*.

do thabairt. I take this to be parallel (cf. *dano*) to *dia chungid*, and *ocus ni...charait* as a parenthesis, suggested by the mention of Conchobar (cf. *o Chonchobar*). Cf. Thurneysen, 'Auch wir sind gekommen, um ihn zu bitten,' sagten die Ulter Boten, 'von Conchobar gesandt. Und Conchobar ist als Freund nicht weniger wert. Auch er wird dir Schätze und Vieh geben und denselben Betrag,' etc. 'We also,' said the heralds from Ulster, 'have come to ask for thy hound; we have been sent by Conor, and Conor is a friend who is of no less value than these. He also will give to thee treasures and cattle, and the same amount at,' etc., which is not very literal. A possible alternative interpretation of LL. would be to regard *dano do thabairt* as parallel to *do charait*, and to translate: 'and Conchobar's value as a friend, and indeed in giving treasure and cattle is no less; and the same amount shall,' etc. For *i cind bliadna* H. 3. 18 has *atuaith*; and Rawl. B. 512 has *atúaid co n-imarcraid fair*, which Meyer transl. '(and the same amount shall be given) from the north, and be added to,' etc. *biaid... de*, lit. 'there will be good friendship from it' (? i.e. from the transaction).

3. *Ro-lá* appears to be used here intransitively; cf. ch. 20, note s.v.

cor-rabi, for *co ro-bói* (for *bói*, 3rd sing. perf. of *bí, bíid*), rel. w. consecutive *co*, lit. 'so that he was.' But *co* is always more than a mere copulative. It may be compared with the Anglo-Saxon conj. *þæt*, perhaps also with the difficult *forþon*, and may best be translated 'and so,' 'and in this way, occasionally 'and as a result.'

tri thráth. Windisch transl. 'hours,' but three hours is not long to abstain from food and sleep, and edd. have translated variously. Leahy om.; Thurneysen, 'zwei volle Tage'; Meyer, 'three days and nights'; Duvau, 'longtemps.' Yet the word commonly means 'hour,' 'canonical hours.' Cf. ch. 12, note s.v. Perhaps here 'three meal-times,' i.e. a whole day. It seems to have come to be used in a general sense in the Med. period. O'Don. Suppl. transl. *tráth* 'time,' 'a natural day of twenty-four hours.' We may cf. with this passage *Bricriu's Feast* (ed. Henderson, I.T.S., ch. x), *nírchotail ocus ni roloing co cend tri lá ocus teóra n-aidche,* 'He neither ate nor slept till the end of three days and three nights' (Henderson).

cen chotlod. cen aspirates a following consonant, which however is only indicated in the case of *c* (Windisch). Om. Harl. 5280.

acht co immorchor. Co, here written for *oc a,* lit. 'but (he was) at his tossing,' i.e. 'But he tossed,' taking *acht* in the sense of 'but.' This use of *acht* with the verbal noun is not uncommon and the construction is regular. Windisch transl. 'he cast himself from one side to the other'; 'but was moving about from one side to another' (Meyer); Thurneysen, 'sondern wälzte sich von einer Seite auf die andere.'

ón táib, ó + dat. of the article + *táib.*

Is...riss, lit. 'It is then spoke his wife to him.' In Mid. Irish *ré* and *re* are sometimes confused. *Re* took the place of *fri,* and combined with the 3rd pers. pron. gave *ris(s).* Cf. Bergin, *Stories from Keating²* (Dublin, 1925), p. xxi; E. Knott, *Bardic Poems of Tadg Dall O'Huiginn,* Introduction, s.v. Prepositional Pronouns.

Is fota...itái, lit. 'It is long the fasting in which you are.' In E.Ir. the rel. pron. is usually om. after the prep. *i n-.* For *itái* Rawl. B. 512 has *atái.*

cen co n-essara, lit. 'without that you eat it'; Rawl. B. 512 has *gen cu hesta,* which Meyer transl. 'though thou wouldst not eat it.' Thurneysen transl. LL. 'Du hast Speise vor dir und issest nicht.'

Cid no-tái, lit. 'What (is it) that you are' (*no* being the preverbal rel. particle), i.e. 'What is it that ails you?'

Ni...mnaí, lit. 'he did not give an answer to the woman.'

conid, 'ut sit' (Windisch); lit. 'so that it is.' For the form cf. Windisch, *Gram.,* § 387; Strachan, *Ériu,* vol. I, part II, p. 56. *co n + id,* i.e. 3rd sing. conjunct. form of the pres. indic. of the copula.

conid...ben, lit. 'so that it is then the woman spoke.' Thurneysen: 'Da sprach sie weiter.' Rawl. B. 512 has *conid ann asbert,* 'and then she said,' (Meyer); 'Whereupon she said' (Leahy). *in ben:* This is possibly a marginal indication of the speaker, like those which follow, and not the subject of *roráid,* though Harl. 5280 makes it more natural to regard *in ben* as the subject. The latter text has *cid notai al in ben nochorus acill. is ann idbert an ben Tucad,* etc.

l. 1. *Tucad*, etc., lit. 'Sleeplessness was brought to M. D. into his house (Meyer, Thurneysen). *Turbaid chotulta*, 'interruption of sleep.'

ros-bói ní, lit. 'There was to him a thing,' i.e. 'he had something.' This would have been *rambói* (*r-an-bói*) in E. Ir. The infixed -*s*- is a M. Ir. development. For *s* as an infixed masc. pron. 3rd. sing., see Strachan, *Ériu*, vol. I, part II, pp. 157, 167; Dottin, *Manuel d'Irlandais moyen*, vol. I, § 312 ff. H. 3. 18 has *baithut in ní* (read *baithut ní*), 'there was to thee a thing.'

l. 3. *Asoí* (*a sui* H. 3. 18). The word is not known elsewhere. *dosoi...fraig* would mean ' He turns from me to the wall.' Windisch suggests *asoí...fraig*, 'he turns away from me and turns to the wall,' and compares *co immorchor ón táib co araile* above. Meyer om. *asoí* in his transl. 'he turns from me to the wall.' So also Thurneysen. Possibly we should read *ad-soí...* 'he turns towards me and from me to the wall,' which would go better with the rest of the context. Cf. however Pedersen, *Vergl. Gram.*, vol. II, § 834 (2).

fene is gen. sing. of *Fían*, but it is doubtful if the reference is to the heroes of the Fenian Cycle. *in ferg fene*, 'the hero of the Fene' (Meyer); 'Der Irenfürst' (Thurneysen). Harl. 5280 reads *feius*. For an account of the *Fíana* and the early history of the word, see Meyer, *Fianaighecht*, p. v ff.

londgail. Om. Windisch Gloss.; 'of fierce valour' (Meyer); 'der grimme Held' (Thurneysen). For *lond* see vocab. s.v.

dos-beir mod. The *s* of *dos-beir* is the 3rd sing. fem. of the infixed pron. perhaps used as a dat.; but the phrase *dobeir mod* occurs in LU. 55b, and LL. 42b without infix. In Middle Irish the use of infixed *s* is exceedingly common where the verb is followed by an accus. Cf. Strachan, *Ériu*, vol. I, part II, pp. 164, 165. Meyer om. and transl. 'His prudent wife observes (that her husband),' etc. Thurneysen, 'Sein kluges Weib bemerkt es wohl (dass der Schlaf),' etc.; cf. Windisch Gloss. s.v. *é*, p. 514, and s.v. *mod*, where he suggests the transl. 'sie gab Acht auf ihn.' But cf. *mod .i. obair*, O'Cl.; *.i. contabairt*, O'Dav. 1258, and *mod .i. gnim* id. 1268; *dober mod don banchuireo*, LL. *Táin Bó Cúalnge* (ed. Windisch), l. 264, LU. *Táin* l. 62 (Strachan, O'Keefe), which appears to mean : 'he puts a troop of women into astonishment.'

bith...chotlud, lit. 'being without sleep to her husband.' 'That her mate is without sleep' (Meyer); 'Dass der Schlaf den Gatten flieht' (Thurneysen).

l. 5. *maith concelar. maith*, adj. used adverbially.

run...athenar. If we keep the reading of LL., I suppose we must transl. the whole phrase 'The secret of a woman is not well concealed, it is not well entrusted to a slave,' or 'a good (thing) is not,' etc. But the construction would not be a natural one and I have followed the reading of Harl. 5280 (and H. 3. 18) with Meyer and Thurneysen. Cf. also Windisch (p. 111) who appears to favour this reading.

l. 7. *Cid...aire.* I am not sure of the meaning of this line, and the text is possibly corrupt. For *mani...aire*, H. 3. 18 has *manit eplad ní airi*; Harl. 5280, *manidebl ni airi*. Meyer transl. 'Why wouldest thou talk to a woman if something were not amiss?' Thurneysen, 'Auch dem Weibe magst du 's sagen, kann dadurch nichts schlimmer werden'; Leahy, lit. 'Why dost thou speak against a woman unless something fails on that account?'—which is not satisfactory. A possible transl. would be: 'Even though thou shouldst say it to a woman, if nothing were to be lost by it, a thing,' etc. The context favours Thurneysen's transl.

ni...aile. I take this to mean 'the thing which your own mind does not go to (reach), the mind of someone else goes to (reaches it).' Windisch regarded *teiti* as a variant of *téit* (cf. *Kurzgefasste Irische Grammatik* (Leipzig, 1879), p. 114). It is, however, more probable that the *-i* of *teiti* is an affixed pron. 3rd sing. neut., and we should therefore transl. 'the mind of someone else goes (to) it,' i.e. penetrates. The latter alternative would account better for the two forms within the same line (*téit, teiti*), which is obviously carefully constructed with the two half-lines artificially balanced. Meyer's transl. perhaps favours the former alternative: 'A thing that the mind will not penetrate, someone else's mind will penetrate.' For *teiti menma*, H. 3. 18 reads *teit a menmai* and Harl. 5280 *teti a menmo*, which are not convincing as the change of construction in the middle of the line is awkward. Thurneysen transl. 'Was du selber nicht ersinnst fällt gar oft dem andern ein.'

l. 9. *ba...dó.* 'Evil was the day when they came for him' (Meyer); 'Wehe, dass man nach ihm sandte' (Thurneysen). For the form *etha* cf. Pedersen, *op. cit.* II, § 716. *ethaid* (3rd sing. pres.) occurs elsewhere with the sense 'he comes.' Windisch compares *atetha* 'he takes,' 'seizes' (perhaps orig. 'he comes to,' 'comes at'). Cf. his Gloss. s.v.

dofaeth. The form is 3rd sing. s.-fut. of *tuitim*, 'I fall.'

mór fer find. Harl. 5280 has *mor bfer bfind. Mór* is neut., *fer* gen. pl., the pronunciation of which is indicated by Harl.

fria rath. Windisch here understood *ráth* 'fortified dwelling.' *Fria ráth* would then be 'to (or possibly 'against') his (? Mesroeda's) abode.' Meyer and Thurneysen were no doubt right however in regarding *rath* as the *rath* which Windisch glosses 'Gnade,' 'gratia'; transl. 'for his sake,' 'on account of.' Cf. *a rath mathiusa*, 'for the sake of good' (Atkinson, Gloss. to the Laws, s.v. *rath*).

bid...chath appears to be metrically defective. For *lia turim* Harl. 5280 has *lia lin turim.* Windisch suggests that the orig. passage may have been *bid lia turim lín a chath*, and transl. s.v. *cath* (nom. sing.) 'das Kämpfen um ihn,' and s.v. *lia* 'der Kämpfe um ihn wird mehr sein als zu zählen.' This suggestion is probably correct, but curiously enough Windisch does not seem to have been aware of the correct reading of Harl. 5280: *b[id] lia lin t[ur]im a cat.* The expression *lia turem*, 'more numerous than can be counted,' is not uncommon however. Cf. *Bricriu's Feast*, § 28, *Is lia turem tra ocus asneis*, 'It would be overmuch to recount and to declare' (Henderson). The text of Harl. would make *cath* gen. pl. and give good sense. Meyer transl. 'More than one can tell will be the fights for him.' *lia* is possibly disyllabic here, however, as indicated in H. 3. 18 *liaa*. Cf. Sommer, *Indogermanische Forschungen*, vol. XI, p. 236 ; Pedersen, II, p. 120.

l. 11. *Manip...berthair*, lit. 'If it be not to Conchobar that it shall be given.' *manip*, i.e. *ma* ('if') + *ni* ('not') + *-p* (3rd sing. pres. subj. conjunct. form of the copula). Cf. O'Connell, *Gram.* § 210.

is...gním. The word *mogda* occurs also in *Saltair na Rann* (Stokes) 5753 ; a derivative from *mug*, 'a slave,' 'servant,' + *-da*, adj. ending. H. 3. 18 has *mogdai*. Meyer transl. 'Certainly it will be a churlish deed'; Thurneysen, 'Fürchterlich seh ich die Folgen'; Leahy, 'He shall deem it the deed of a churl.' I suggest that possibly Mesroeda's fear is that Conor will degrade him to the status of a *mug* (cf. *no...thír*).

no con...thír. Windisch, 'Seine Schaaren werden nichts mehr von Rindern oder von Land übrig lassen.' Meyer, 'His hosts will not leave any more of cattle or of land.' The exact bearing of *mó* appears to me uncertain. Thurneysen transl. freely 'meine Rinder, meine Länder—nichts verschonen seine Heere.' *no con*, the emphatic neg. freq. employed in Mid. Irish in the emphatic position of the principal clause. The older form is *ní co(n)*, lit. 'not at all.' Cf. *ni con fes* below. See Pedersen, *op. cit.*, vol. II, § 528 ; Thurneysen, *Handbuch des Alt-Irischen*, I, *Grammatik*, § 851 ff. Can the sentence as a whole mean that Conor's hosts will not leave behind them anything of greater value than the dog (in spite of their promises)? If, however, the preceding line means, as I think not improbable, that technical degradation ensues when an inferior refuses a request to a superior, *no...thír* must refer to the consequent confiscations.

na: I think that this is probably the M. Ir. form of E. Ir. *indá, andá*, 'than.' Earlier edd. however appear to regard it as M. Ir. form of E. Ir. *nó*, 'or.' Cf. note above.

l. 13. *Mad*, a compound of *ma*, 'if,' with the 3rd sing. pres. conjunct. of the copula. For a suggested derivation, see Thurneysen, *Ir. Gram.* § 786; cf. Windisch, *Kurzgefasste Irische Grammatik*, § 387 (transl. Engl. Norman Moore).

falmag. According to Meyer this is the *mag* ('plain') of *Fál*, one of the poet. names for Ireland. Cf. *Inisfáil*. See ed. cited p. 58[2]. So also Thurneysen, who translates:

> 'Wag ich Ailill abzuweisen,
> Stürzt sich Irland auf mein Volk.'

These explanations are not convincing, however, and the lines are unintelligible as they stand. The first element in *falmag* is not uncommon. Cf. *fálbach .i. fál abach nó fál corp* (O'Clery), 'a heap of corpses.' Cf. further *falgis falbaigi móra de chollaib a bid bad, Táin Bó Cúalnge*, ed. Windisch, l. 2649.

Mad...túaith. This half-line does not make sense as it stands. Windisch suggested that the reading *silis* be adopted from H. 3. 18 and Harl. 5280. *silis* is the reduplicating s.-fut. of *sligid*, 'he hews.' Harl. 5280 is actually written *era si lis*, which we might regard as 2nd sing. of the verb *eraim*,

'I refuse.' The chief objection to this seems to me to be the awkwardness of the use of the 2nd sing. here. This is obviated if we regard the whole passage from *manip...immi* (6 ll.) as spoken by the woman—an arrangement which seems to me preferable. No indication of the speaker is given throughout the poem in Harl. 5280 or in H. 3. 18. We may perhaps translate: 'If to Ailill thou refusest him (or, if there is a refusal to Ailill) he will hew down a heap of corpses across the country.' The line *mad do Ailill* is a syllable short, however. For *era* cf. Pedersen, *op. cit.* § 834 (5).

dar sin túaith. See above. Harl. 5280 reads *tiarstituaid*; H. 3. 18 *tair sa tuaith.*

do-don-béra, 3rd sing. fut. of *dobiur* with infixed pron. 1st pl. *-aon* Thurneysen keeps the reading of LL. 'Matas Sohn führt uns hinweg'; Meyer accepts the reading of H. 3. 18 *do notberai* with infixed pron. 3rd sing. *-t-,* '(The son of Mata) will carry it off.' Harl. 5280 has *donobéra.*

ata...lúaith, obscure. Thurneysen reads *ata-nebla i luim luaith.* Meyer om. The text is possibly corrupt. H. 3. 18 has *ataneplai lomm luaith*; Harl. 5280 *adanebla aloim luaid, atanepla* for *ad-don-ebla,* 'he will drive (i.e. crush) us'? Cf. Pokorny, *Hist. Reader of O. Ir.,* p. 35.

l. 15. *Tathut...lim-sa,* lit. 'It is to thee with me,' i.e. 'I have for thee.' Cf. O'Connell, *Grammar of Old Irish* (Belfast, 1912), § 87; Thurneysen, *Gram.* § 428 (3). The form *táthut* is commonly found in poetry.

ris for *fris,* i.e. (*f*)*ri* + 3rd sing. pron. masc. and neut. (cf. O'Connell, *Gram.* § 89). Windisch transl. here 'dazu' or 'dagegen'; Meyer, 'I have advice for thee in this.' Thurneysen, 'Einen Rat hab ich für dich.'

ní holc...ninni. Meyer transl. 'The result of which will not be bad'; Thurneysen, 'der die schlimmen Folgen hebt.' For *ninni* H. 3. 18 has *n-intti,* Harl. 5280 *ninde.* The meaning however seems to be: 'We (women—I) are not bad at directing (*sc.* an affair).' *Ninni* is the form of the 1st pl. pron. used after *is.* See Thurneysen, *Gram.* § 404. For *iarmairt* cf. Mod. Ir. *iarmairt,* 'issue of an affair' (E. I. *airmbert*).

cumma...immi. Meyer transl. 'No matter who will fall for it'; Thurneysen, 'Mögen sie sich drum erschlagen,' which is rather free; Leahy, 'and who dies for it little we care.' *Cumma,* 'alike' (? in regard to us). 'No matter who should fall on account of it.' Cf. Mod. Ir. *is cumma liom,* 'it is a matter of indifference to me.'

17. *doberi-siu.* Windisch points out (see his Gloss. s.v. *dobiur*) that *doberi* ought to be written *dobir* or *dobeir* (conjunct. forms). *Beri* is the absolute. Cf. Thurneysen, *Gram.* § 553; O'Connell, *Gram.* § 176. The form in LL. gives the line a syllable too many. Harl. 5280 and H. 3. 18 read *tabair.*

isi...cutal, obscure. Meyer transl. 'It does not make me glad'; Thurneysen, 'der befreit mich von der Sorge.' *Cutal* is a rare word which is glossed *saoth, olc.* Cf. O'Clery, Gloss. (Meyer, *Contributions to Irish Lexicography,* Halle, 1906, s.v.). Cf. O'Mulc. 757 *cutal caille,* 'a blind nut,' 'an empty shell,' also ib. 257 (*Archiv* I, 246). The word may however be miswritten for *cuthal .i. tláith* (?'feeble' Meyer) O'Mulc. Gloss. *Archiv* I. *Deni* is 3rd sing. pres. indic.

of *dénim.* *Ním,* the neg. *ní*+1st pers. pron., lit. 'It is it that does not leave
me without resource,' or perhaps 'make me feeble,' i.e. 'it is helpful to me.'
H. 3. 18 has *isí nindene cutal.* Harl. 5280 *es hí nim dena.*

Ailbe...dia. This half-line is believed to be corrupt; om. Meyer. Thurneysen, 'Ailbe, ihn hat Gott gesandt' (taking *Día,* 'God'). *Do-roid* is perf. of
do-fóidi, 'sends along,' and the meaning appears to be 'God has sent him
along.'

ni...tucad. The exact bearing of the line is uncertain owing chiefly to the
obscurity of the preceding half-line. *tucad* will hardly bear Leahy's transl.
'There is no-one who can tell whence he sprung.' Windisch transl. 'von
wem er davon getragen worden ist'; Meyer, 'It is not known by whom it
was given'; Thurneysen, 'niemand weiss von wem er kam.'

4. *nom-bertaigedar,* so Harl. 5280; LL. reads *ro-*. I do not feel certain about
this form either here or in ch. 15 q.v. The left stroke of the first letter in
LL. runs below the line, but the form of the verb (3rd sing. pres. indic.
depon.) suggests *no-*. LL. is very indistinct in the whole passage here (but
not in ch. 15) and *r* may be a badly written *n* or a scribal error. I prefer
to assume the former, on the authority of the other texts, rather than to
emend the verb to a pret. form (cf. *rom-bertaigestar,* ch. 15) as would be
natural if we read *ro.* H. 3. 18 *nosmbertaigter*; Rawl. B. 512 *nosbertaigenn*
'gives himself a shake' (Meyer); Thurneysen, 'reckte sich.' For the infixed
pronouns here cf. Dottin, *Manuel d'Irlandais moyen,* vol. I, § 211; Strachan,
Ériu, vol. I, part II, p. 165 f. *nom-bertaigedar,* from *no-an-bertai-gedar,* lit.
'gives himself a shake.'

Bad...dodn-ancatar. lit. 'Now let (there be) good to us,' said he, 'and to
the guests who have come to us.' *maith,* so Windisch, Leahy. Thurneysen
'guter Dinge.' He transl. the whole: 'So lasst uns und die Gäste, die nach
ihm gesandt sind, guter Dinge sein.' Rawl. B. 512 has *Tabraid bíad tra
or sé co m-ba maith dún,* 'Now bring us food' saith he, 'and let us and the
guests who have come here be merry' (Meyer).

gairmter...Connacht. Om. H. 3. 18 and Rawl. B. 512, which read *teit leo for
leith,* 'he went (lit. 'goes') aside with them' (Meyer); Harl. 5280 has *tet leis
for leith .i. lia techt Connacht.*

co ro-glé dam. The force of *glé* is not certain here. Cf. vocab. s.v. *-glé.*
Windisch suggested that *glé* may here be used intrans., 'until it became clear
to me.' Rawl. B. 512 reads *conidh edh rofás desidhe co tartus in coin,* etc.
Meyer transl. 'and this is what has grown of it'; Thurneysen, 'bis ich zum
Entschluss kam.' The text of H. 3. 18 gives earlier *condergli .i. diratus-sai,*
etc.; Harl. 5280, *7 a comtabairt co ro gleus an comtapairt sen .i. deradusa in
coin do Ailill 7 do Medb asan cuñtauairt sen.*

doratusa, lit. 'I have given.' The change of construction is common in
Irish, the *.i.* introducing the phrase which is in reality the subject of the
verb in the previous phrase, or else which amplifies the idea contained in
the subject.

tecat (3rd pl. imper.). Rawl. B. 512 and Harl. 5280 read *tecait* (a Mid. Ir. form) which Meyer transl. 'Let them come.'

co sochraid. The other MSS. add *ocus co huallach*, 'splendidly and proudly' (Meyer).

ros-bia, lit. 'There shall be to them'; preverbal particle *ro* + infixed pron. 3rd pl. *-s-* + 3rd sing. fut. of *tá*. For other parallel forms cf. O'Connell, *Gram.* § 85; Dottin, *Manuel*, I, § 312 ff.

biad. Harl. 5280 adds 7 *ascetai.*

ocus...dóib, lit. 'and it is welcome they are.'

Buidig...athesc. H. 3. 18, *buidhigh side da*[*no*]. So also Harl. 5280. Om *techta...athesc* H. 3. 18 and Harl. 5280. Rawl. B. 512 reads *Tíagait ass na teachta sin 7 robtar buidigh*, 'Those messengers go out and were thankful (Meyer).

Doratusa...coin, lit. 'I have given,' said he, 'from my hesitation, the hound,' etc. Meyer transl. 'After much doubting I have given the hound'; Leahy, 'After long hesitation I have awarded the hound'; Thurneysen, 'nach langem Schwanken hab ich,' etc. *As* here, 'as a result of.'

bid, so LL. H. 3. 18 has *ba* (subj.); Harl. 5280 has *bad* (imper.); Rawl. B. 512 *do Conchobar 7 ticed co huallach ar a cend 7 formna in cóicidh*, 'and let him and the flower of the province come for it proudly' (Meyer). Probably we should read *bed* (*bad*) *uallach tiastar*, 'let it be proudly he shall come.'

Bertait ascada, or? 'They shall bring'; Windisch transl. 'Sie sollen Geschenke bringen'; Thurneysen, 'Sie werden Geschenke erhalten'; Leahy, 'They shall have presents.' H. 3. 18 has *ascaid uile*; Rawl. B. 512 has *berait aisceda imda eili 7 roforbia failti*, 'and they shall have many other gifts' (Meyer). Possibly the *ascada* are the presents offered from Conchobar by the messengers in ch. 2.

Budig...Ulad, om. in the other MSS.

5. *oen*, here 'the same.'

ro-dalait-seom, a M.Ir. pass. formation. H. 3. 18 and Harl. 5280 read *ro-dalsat-som* (intransitive), which is better: 'Now for one day they made their tryst'; Rawl. B. 512 *rodáilest*[*ur*] *som íat uili*, 'He had made his tryst with them all.' Windisch expands *et* into *etir* and transl. 'von Ost und West.' The whole sentence would then read, 'They met together from east and west on the same day.' This is a not unusual use of *etir*. Perhaps we should understand: 'For the same day they made an agreement among themselves, (he and) the men from the East and the men from the West.' Meyer and Thurneysen both take Mac Dathó to be subject. Meyer, 'But for one and the same day he had made his tryst with them all'; Thurneysen, 'Er hatte aber beide...auf denselben Tag bestellt,' evidently adopting the reading of Harl. 5280 which omits *et*.

Ni...da[*no*], lit. 'Moreover it was not neglected by them.'

cóiced, lit. a 'fifth,' i.e. one of the five provinces of Ireland. In the Heroic Age, the five provinces comprised, according to Keating, Ulster, Connaught

Leinster, and two provinces of Munster. According to Irish tradition (cf. e.g. Keating, vol. II, p. 245, Irish Texts Society) about the second century A.D. Tuathal Techtmhar is said to have founded the kingdom of Meath by cutting off contiguous pieces from Ulster, Munster, Connaught and Leinster. Of the *cóiced* or province of Meath with the seat of the high kingship of Tara the *Táin Bó Cúalnge* knows nothing. It is probably to the earlier divisions that our text refers here. Cf. however *i n-iarthor Mide*, ch. 1, and see E. MacNeill, *Phases of Irish History*, ch. 4.

Ni ro-bar-fachlisem, so LL. Harl. 5280 has *robofaclemur*; H. 3. 18, *ni farcelsam*. Om. Rawl. B. 512; Thurneysen transl. 'Auf zwei Heere auf einmal waren wir nicht vorbereitet'; Leahy, 'For two armies at the same time we were not prepared.' The form in LL. is a late perf. of *fuciallathar*, 'expects.' See Pedersen, § 678 (4). *Bar* (the poss. pron. 2nd pl.) is in M. Ir. used for the infixed pron. 2nd pl. See Atkinson, *Passions and Homilies*, Gloss. s.v. ; Strachan, *Ériu*, vol. I, pp. 158, 160 f.

ar apaide, for *ar a apa-ide*, or *ar a abba-ide*, 'for its reason,' 'however,' 'nevertheless.' Cf. Meyer, *Contributions*, s.v. *abba* (*apa*), 'cause,' and for exx. see Windisch, Gloss. to the *Táin Bó C.* Harl. 5280 reads *ol se arabaidi is*, etc. Rawl. B. 512 *Is mochen duib, a óca, olsé. Táitidh amuigh isin less*, ' 'Tis welcome ye are, O warriors,' saith he. 'Come within into the close' (Meyer).

mo chen. Stokes suggests that this is for *m'fochen* (*mo fochen*). The same phrase occurs in *Broccan's Hymn* (ed. Windisch, *Irische Texte*, p. 40, l. 23). Meyer, however, keeps *cen* f. 'affection,' and appears to regard *mo-chen, fo-chen* as analogous forms (cf. *Contributions*, s.v. 1 *cen*). The phrase *mo chen duib*, whatever its origin, is very common, even in eighteenth-century texts, and is generally transl. 'My love to you.' Cf. Oıᵭe Ċloınne Uıᵲnıᵹ (Dublin, 1914). Meyer translates the passage in our text, ''Tis welcome ye are'; Thurneysen, 'Heiss ich euch willkommen.'

less, cf. vocab. s.v. In spite of the frequent occurrence of the word in the sagas the meaning has never been precisely ascertained, so far as I am aware. According to O'Curry (*Manners and Customs of the Ancient Irish* (1873), vol. III, p. 4) the *less* or *lis* was the same as the *ráth*, but more especially some kind of fortification formed of earth. Sometimes however the word appears to be used in a more general sense.

Nir-bo for *ni-ro-bo*, 'was not.'

Niptar, for *ni-ptar* (*batar*) 3rd pl. pret. indic. conjunct. form of the copula, 'They were not.'

Niptar...araile. Rawl. B. 512 has *Nírbo heinighi carat cach im fleid in lucht bátar isin tigh sin, uair sochaide dib rofuáchenaig fri araile .i. tri chét bliadan ria n-gein críst bái cocad etorra*, 'Those were not faces of friends at a feast, the people who were in that house, for many of them had injured another; for 300 years before the birth of Christ there had been war between them' (Meyer).

Sochaide...araile. Meyer transl. 'For many of them had injured another';

I think it means that hostilities had taken place. Harl. 5280 has *soctus dib roractnaich fri eroili.*

Marbthair, 3rd sing. pass. pres., so Windisch and Thurneysen; H. 3. 18 and Rawl. B. 512 have *marbthar,* conjunct. form. Meyer, 'Let the pig be killed for them.'

bliadan. Windisch expands the *bl.* of LL. to the late form of gen. pl. commonly found in MSS. The earlier form would be *bliadne.* Cf. Meyer, *Contributions,* s.v.

Tri neim, 'through poison.' H. 3. 18 and Harl. 5280 read *tré nemh* (M. Ir. form). Thurneysen, 'Aber mit Gift muss es genährt worden sein.' *Neim* is acc. sing. Cf. Windisch, Gloss. s.v. Rawl. B. 512 reads *tria neimh,* 'On venom that pig had been reared' (Meyer).

no-bíata[r]. So MS. LL., 3rd sing. rel. pres. indic. pass. of *biathaim.* Better, *no-bíata* on the authority of Harl. 5280 (for *biath-ta*) 3rd sing. imperf. pass. H. 3. 18 has *biadta.* See vocab. s.v. *biathaim.* Meyer expands *biath* of Rawl. B. 512 to *bíathad,* 3rd sing. pret. pass. Cf. note above.

co ro-lathea, 3rd sing. pass. subj. corres. to *ro-lá,* suppl. verb to *cuir* (Pedersen, II, § 697), 'it so befell that.'

6. *dia tarsnu. Di* prob. for *do. Tarsnu* is not a common word. O'Reilly glosses it together with *tarsin, tarsa.* Rawl. B. 512 has *dia tarraing na hénmuici,* '(60 oxen) drawing the one pig' (Meyer); H. 3. 18 has 7 *cethracha dam dia odu.* Thurneysen transl. 'und vierzig Ochsen als Unterlage'; Leahy takes *dia tarsnu* lit. 'crosswise to it,' yet transl. '40 oxen as side-dishes to it.' We may, however, cf. *tarsand,* 'relish,' 'condiment' (*Archiv,* I, pp. 263, 321); acc. pl. *torsnu, Aisl. M. Congl.* 196, 'sauces' (Meyer); *tri tharsunn* (Triads). The orig. may have been *dia tarsū,* i.e. *tarsun,* and misread *tarsnu.*

icond ferdaigsecht, 'at the stewardship.' Cf. vocab. s.v. *oc.* Rawl. B. 512 reads *oc á feirthigis,* lit. 'at their steward' (i.e. 'was attending on them'). Cf. Pedersen, § 805 (note).

Mo chen. Cf. 5 above.

ni...Laigniu. This sentence is not easy if read without a stop as Windisch prints. The punctuation in our text is suggested by Meyer (*Hibernica Minora* (Oxford, 1894), p. 52, footnote 4). After *frisin* (LL. *riss sin*) Rawl. B. 512 adds *cutruma m-bíd sin,* 'and there is not to be found the like of such a quantity of food' (Meyer). *Ni...sin* may however be lit. 'not comparing you (i.e. your eating capacity) to that,' i.e. 'I am not going to put you off with so little as that.' Cf. *condan-samailter fri cech ndodcadchai,* Milan Glosses, 63 d. 7 (in *Thes. Pal.,* ed. Stokes and Strachan).

Ataat...Laigniu, lit. 'There are bullocks and pigs with the men of Leinster.' Rawl. B. 512 reads *Ataat muca imda 7 aighi la Laighniu,* 'We have many pigs and beeves in Leinster.' H. 3. 18, *Atat aighe 7 mucai la L.*

A testa desin, 'was davon fehlt' (Windisch). *desin,* i.e. *di sin.* After *a testa* Rawl. B. 512 reads *dá bhar m-bíathad anocht,* 'to your provision tonight' (Meyer).

imbárach. After *amárach* (for *imbárach*) Rawl. B. 512 reads '*Is maith in bíathad,*' *ar Conchob*[*ar*]. *Nónbar im*[*morro*] *robái fón cleith for a raibe tarr na muici* 7 *bái a n-eiri and* '*Is maith in muc,*' etc. 'The provision is good, saith Conchobar. There were nine men under the hurdle on which was the tail of the pig, and they had their load therein. 'The pig is good,' etc.

Cinnas. Rawl. B. 512 here inserts *is áil duib a roind,* 'How would ye fain divide it?' (Meyer).

anuas ane, obscure. *induas amne as an imda,* Harl. 5280; H. 3. 18 has *anuas amne asind imdai.* Windisch accordingly suggests emend. *ane* to *amne,* adv. 'so,' 'thus,' here and in ch. 12. Rawl. B. 512 has here merely *anúas asin imdaidh,* 'out of his chamber above' (Meyer). Is this 'chamber' to be identified with the *grianán* mentioned in *Bricriu's Feast* (ed. Henderson), ch. 13?

bale. Cf. vocab. Meyer here appears to regard *bale* as used adverbially. He transl. ' Where the valorous warriors,' etc. See below.

láith gaile, 'heroes of valour.'

Cinnas...chomramaib, lit. 'How (shall it be divided, cf. above) in the place in which are the warriors of valour of the men of Ireland except by dividing according to brave deeds,' etc. For *ar galaib ocus ar chomramaib* Rawl. B. 512 has *ar comromaib gaiscid,* 'by contest of arms' (Meyer). Thurneysen, following our text, transl. 'Wie?' rief Br. C's Sohn von oben herab; 'da wo die Kämpen der Iren versammelt sind, nur nach Massgabe seiner Waffenthaten und Kämpfe!'

dorat...dib. The order in Harl. 5280 and H. 3. 18 is *dorat cach dib buille,* 'Each of you has given a blow.' So Thurneysen and Leahy. Rawl. B. 512, *doratt cach díb builli,* 'Let each of you give' (Meyer).

riam, etc. Rawl. B. 512 has *dar sroin araile ár sin,* 'on the other's nose' (Meyer). *Riam, ré* (*n-*) with neut. pron. 'before it,' 'before this.' *a cheile,* 'each other,' here used as a reciprocal pronoun.

istaig, prep. *i*(*n*)+neut. dat. sing. of the article *sind*+dative of the noun. The contracted form *is* for *isind* is not a phonetic development, but appears to have been influenced by the form *istech* (contracted from *i-sa tech*). Cf. ch. 15, note s.v., and see Pedersen, I, § 170.

ro-imthigitar. H. 3. 18 has *imrulatar;* Harl. 5280, *imrulát.* Thurneysen transl. the whole passage, 'So ziemt sichs,' stimmte C. bei. 'Haben wir doch Bursche genug hier im Haus, die das Grenzland durchstreift haben'; Leahy, ' We have here a plenty of lads in this house who have done battle on the borders.' Rawl. B. 512 has *roimthigset in coicrích mór fecht,* 'We have lads in the house that have many a time gone round the border' (Meyer).

7. *Ricfait*[*er*], etc. See vocab. s.v. The meaning required seems to be, 'You will come upon (i.e. discover) the profit (i.e. value) of your young men.' Rawl. B. 512 has *ricfit*[*er*], etc. 'There will be need of thy lads to-night' (Meyer). Thurneysen transl. 'Du wirst sie heut Abend nötig haben, deine Bursche'; Leahy, 'Thou shalt lose thy lads tonight.' The expression *recam-ni*

a les em ar curaid occurs in *Bricriu's Feast*, ch. 56, where Windisch transl. 'Wir brauchen unsere Helden,' but with doubt as to the construction, which seems to be parallel to the one in our text. Henderson transl. 'We really require our heroes.' The *a* before *les* is the possess. pron. 3rd pl. used in anticipation.

This chapter contains an account of the boasting which is commonly found at heroic banquets. Cf. p. 7 above. It will be noted that in this chapter the boasting is indiscriminate and not, as in the subsequent ordeals, concentrated on one or two central figures. Indeed, the matter seems to lie here among heroes of Munster stock (see names in Index) and not to follow any of the well-worn catalogues. Cf. ch. 9 note s.v. *Loegaire.*

Arad. Rawl. B. 512 reads *senlaech amra*, 'a famous old warrior' (Meyer). Harl. 5280 has *senlagh.*

al-luachraib. Harl. 5280 has *a cruacn.*; H. 3. 18 and Rawl. B. 512 have *a Cruachnaib.* If Windisch is correct in keeping the reading of LL., which is not uncommon in place-names (cf. Hogan s.v. *Lúachair*), we must understand *al-* for *ess, a, á* (prep.) with doubling of foll. cons., 'from the rushes of Conalaid.' Thurneysen transl. 'aus dem Conalad-Röhricht,' and below *a Cruachnaib Conalad*, 'von den Conalad-Hügeln.' Rawl. B. 512 reads *C(rui)thne* for *Cruachniu.*

Ba...tóin. The words *rota* and *fó tóin* are obscure. Meyer transl. *rota* by 'roads.' Lit. 'It has happened often to you to leave a fat bullock of your party with me.' MSS. vary considerably in their readings. H. 3 18 has *Ba menic roda Luachra Dedad lim-sa fa toin. Menic agh meit d'agbail daib agam-sa.* So also Harl. 5280 (*fo a toin*); Rawl. B. 512, *Bá meinic roda Luachra Dedad for a tóin. Ba meinic agh meith do fácbail lim-sa beos*, 'The roads of Luachair Dedad have often had their backs turned to them. Many a fat beeve too have they left with me' (Meyer). The *ag méth* is probably figurative, and *fó tóin* contracted from *fo a tóin* (*a*, possess. adj. Cf. variant readings).

Ba méthiu...fadéin. After *ocain-ni* (*againde*) H. 3. 18 inserts *ar Muindremair mac Gerrgind.* Harl. 5280 reads *ba menciu letsai ag met dacb. ocaind ar Munremur m. Gerginn m. Illodan m. Oingusa b.m. Rudri. am foracbois do braitir bdein*; Rawl. B. 512, *fa méith in t-ag f[or]facbais-siu lim-sa ol Muinremar mac Geirrgind.*

Cruachniu...Conalad. H. 3. 18, *Cruaichne mac Ruadluim a Cruachnaib*; Harl. 5280, *Cruaicniu mac Ruadluim a Cruacn. Conal.*; Rawl. B. 512, *C[rui]thne mac Rúaidlinde a Cruachnaib Connacht.* Cf. note above s.v. *al-luachraib.*

andás, the rel. form of 3rd sing. of this cpd. of *-táu* is used where we should use 'than' after a compar., i.e. 'better...than is Loth,' etc.; from compar. particle *in* (*an*) + *-táas, -tás* (from *táim*), 'more than is,' 'beyond what is.'

Cinnas fir lib. I take this to be the idiomatic use of *le* to express opinion— *lib*, 'in your opinion.' 'What sort of a man do you think him?' (Meyer).

Thurneysen and Leahy understand it rather differently, taking *líb*, 'whom you speak of,' 'Was sagt ihr denn dazu?' (Thurneysen); 'What sort of a man was he whom you boast of?' (Leahy). More probably we should read *fír*, lit. 'How is this true (or 'proper') in your eyes?' etc. For the use of *fír* here and elsewhere in the saga cf. *Revue Celtique*, vol. XXIV, p. 121 ff.

a chend...de, lit. 'his head to strike (i.e. for striking) from him.'

8. *Immo-tarla...hErend*. Windisch transl. *immo-tarla* (for *imn-a-tarla*) (impers.) 'es kam ihnen dahin dass.' He thinks that the infixed or affixed (cf. *imma tarla*) pron. 3rd sing. *a(n-)* is contained in such forms, often with a sense of opposition (cf. Gloss. p. 515, col. 1). Thurneysen evidently thinks the same, for he transl. 'So kamen sie schliesslich hart an einander, bis ein Mann sich über die Männer Irlands erhob.' He evidently takes *tarla* in a more concrete sense than Windisch (cf. Windisch's Gloss. s.v.). Rawl. B. 512 is different here : *Immátormailt cách díb a chomrama a n-agaid araile, co ríacht fodeóid cusin oenfer robris for cach*, 'Each of them brought up his exploits in the face of the other, till at last it came to one man who beat everyone' (Meyer). For this passage and what follows see introduction, p. 7 above. Such altercations are mentioned by Athenaeus as a recognised accompaniment of the feast among the ancient Gauls. *in t-oinfer*. The def. art. here, as frequently in E.Ir., suggests that the person indicated is going to figure largely in what follows.

Matach. Other MSS. here insert *do Connachtaib*.

Do-fúargaib, etc., or possibly, 'Indeed he raised his weapons above him higher than the weapons of the host,' a transl. which would account better for *fair*. Rawl. B. 512 is simpler, *Túarcaib side im[morro] a gaisced don t-slúaig*, 'He raised his prowess over the host.' H. 3. 18, *difurgaib side im[moro] a gaiscced uas gaiscedaib in tsluaigh*. Thurneysen transl. 'Der hing seine Waffen höher als die Waffen der Menge'; Leahy, 'He hung up his weapons at a greater height than the weapons of anyone else who was there.' Thurneysen considers this as a sign of preeminence in prowess. The phrase occurs in *Bricriu's Feast*, ch. 68, where Henderson transl. 'Cuchullain's valour to rank above that of everyone else.' I think that the phrase refers to boasting, which is a universal accompaniment of heroic banquets.

tairismi, gen. of the verb. n. of *tairissem* (see vocab. and cf. ch. 17 note s.v. *laech a thairismi*). Windisch suggests emend. to *tairissem* to supply the subject to *fagabar*, and compares the phrase *in comram do thairisem beus... no in mucc do raind dam*, ch. 11 f. He regards the verb. n. *lécud* as supplying a second subject to *fagabar*, which is improbable. The lit. meaning seems to be : 'Let the men of Ireland maintain the contest ; otherwise (it will be a case of) surrender of the pig for carving to me.' Thurneysen transl. 'Jetzt soll sich ein irischer Mann finden,' sagte er, 'der den Wettstreit mit mir aufnimmt, oder man lasse mich das Schwein zerlegen.' Harl. 5280 supplies *oinfer* (*tairisme*). Scarre's ed. of H. 3. 18 has *cen* (sic) *fer tairisme comramae frim-sai no legad na muici do roind damh*. Rawl. B. 512, '*Fogabar tra do feraib Er*[*enn*],' *ol se*, '*oenfer tairisme comroma dam-sa, nó léicid in muic do roinn dam*,' 'Now let there be found among the men of Ireland,' saith he, 'one man to abide contest with me, or let me divide the pig.'

nam-mucci, for *na* (gen. sing. fem. of article) + doubling of initial cons. of *mucci*. Cf. O'Connell, *Gram.* § 16.

9. *Ros-lá...h-Ulto*, lit. 'It struck them, the Ultonians, into silence,' i.e. 'silence fell upon the U.' -*s*- is the infixed pron. 3rd pl. used redundantly. Cf. Dottin, *Manuel d'Irlandais moyen*, vol. I, § 314; Strachan, *Eriu*, vol. I, part II, pp. 164 f., 168 f. Rawl. B. 512 and Harl. 5280 omit *s*. Before this passage Rawl. B. 512 inserts *ni frith in tan sin láech a tairisme ag Ulltaib*, 'There was not at that time found a warrior with the men of Ulster to stand up to him' (Meyer); Harl. 5280 *ni frith laegh a tairissme ro lae a socht na hUllto*; H. 3. 18 *ni frith laoch a tairisme*.

Loegaire. In this and the following chapters the boasting, unlike that in ch. 7 which is less formal, takes the form of challenging a central figure. It will be observed that the heroes who challenge Cet are almost all to be found in the catalogue of Ulster champions who are described by Mac Roth and Fergus Mac Roich to Ailill and Medb as they view the Ulster forces from a point of vantage, no doubt on the Hill of Slane. Cf. *Táin Bó Cúalnge* (transl. Dunn), pp. 313 ff. Leahy aptly compares (*Heroic Romances of Ireland*, vol. I, p. 173) the preoccupation with the details of the wounds inflicted by Cet on his enemies with that displayed in similar cases in Homeric combats. It will be observed that Cet never inflicts the same kind of wound twice.

Ni ba fír. Ba is fut. Cf. vocab. s.v.; lit., 'this will not be right'; 'It shall not be' (Meyer); 'Dazu wirds nicht kommen' (Thurneysen); 'Never shall it be' (Leahy). *fír* has prob. the same sense here as in *cinnas fír*, ch. 7 above.

ar ar m-belaib-ni, lit. 'before our lips,' i.e. 'before our noses.' -*ni*, enclitic pron. of 1st pl. *ar belaib*, 'before,' 'in front,' 'in preference to' (O'Donovan, *Gram.* p. 289). Cf. *ar mo chind-sa*, ch. 13.

An bic, for E. Ir. *an biuc*, 'wait a little.' So also H. 3. 18. Rawl. B. 512 reads *mall biuc*, 'wait a little.'

co rot-acilliur. Rawl. B. 512, *co romgladathar-sa*, 'that thou mayst speak to me.'

Is...n-Ultaib, lit. 'There is a custom to you Ultonians.' Cf. *Ériu*, VI, p. 90 ff.

is...báire. Báire, 'the game of hurling,' 'playing-field,' 'goal.' Meyer transl. the passage, 'It is a custom with you Ulstermen that every youth among you who takes arms makes us his first goal,' presumably taking *cend* in the sense of 'end,' 'objective'; but the use with *báire* is certainly awkward. Perhaps *cend a báire* is used here in the sense, 'the goal he aims at.' Thurneysen transl. 'Jeder Knabe...sein erstes Waffenspiel gegen uns spielt'; Leahy, 'Each lad...should play first with us the game of war.'

Dochua[i]daisiu. LL. reads *dochuaicaisiu.* The *c* is a scribal error for *d.*
Harl. 5280 *docodhaise*; H. 3. 18 *dochuad[ais]*.

Imma-tarraid, so Windisch; Thurneysen, 'Wir gerieten dort an einander';
Meyer, 'we met.' *-tarraid,* from *to-air-réth.* Cf. Pedersen, II, § 797 (2).

foracbais...heocho. Rawl. B. 512 reads *Curfácbaisi in t-ara 7 in carpat 7
na heochu lim-sa,* 'thou didst leave charioteer and chariot and horses with
me' (Meyer).

Nis...innasin. The word *toirchi* is not known to me elsewhere. Windisch
suggests connection with *torgim,* 'I come.' Meyer, 'Thou wilt not get at
the pig in that manner'; Thurneysen, 'So kommst du nicht zum Schwein.

Dessid...dano. Rawl. B. 512 has *Deisidh Loeg[airi] ina šuidhe ina lebaid,*
' Lóigaire sat down on his couch' (Meyer).

10. *Ni...imdai.* Rawl. B. 512 reads '*Ní bá fír ón,*' or *óclach find mór do
Ulltaib,* '*Cet do roinn na muici,*' *oc tuidecht anúas asan imdaid,* 'It shall not
be,' saith a tall fair warrior of Ulster, coming out of the chamber above,
'that Cet divide the pig.' The exact meaning of *anúas assind imdai* is not
clear. Cf. ch. 2, note s.v. Thurneysen transl. 'indem er von der Pritsche
vortrat'; 'stepping forward from the bench whereon he had sat' (Leahy).

Is...andaisiu, lit. 'He is better as a hero than thou art.' The complement
of the compar. and superl. of adjectives is frequently introduced by *do*
(older *de*) followed by the dative in Middle Irish. *Andaisiu,* a later form
of *indáisiu.* Cf. ch. 7 s.v. *andás*; Windisch, *Gram.* §§ 186, 187; Thurneysen,
§ 758.

Cid diata, i.e. 'what is it from which is (*di,* 'from,' *-atá-,* 'is'),' i.e. 'why
is?' The phrase *cid dia* is commonly used in the sense of 'whence,' and
cid diatá + a proper name + *for* is a regular idiom for 'why is *x* so-called?'
Cid...athair-siu, lit. 'Why is Lám G. on your father,' i.e. why is he so-called?
Cf. Windisch, *Gram.* § 216 f., and his Gloss. s.v. *cid.*

Ro-fetar-sa. *-fetar* is a pret. or perf. with pres. meaning and cannot
be used without a preceding particle.

do-roich...Lám. Thurneysen transl. 'Alles eilte herbei. Auch Hand kam';
Leahy, 'All men attacked me and Lama Gabaid was among them.' Rawl.
B. 512 reads *conamtarraid Lamguba a cumma cáich,* 'Hand-wail came up
with me like everyone else' (Meyer).

Dos-leicim-se, 'I sent it at him.' Again we have the pleonastic or proleptic
infixed pron. 3rd sing. *-s-.* Cf. ch. 9 note s.v. *ros-lá.*

co...lár. Rawl. B. 512 reads *coraib hi isind achad ina fiadnaisi,* 'so that
it was on the field before him' (Meyer).

Cid...frim-sa, or possibly this may mean : 'What is it his son would offer
me in the way of combat?' Thurneysen transl. 'Was sollte seinen Sohn zum
Wettstreit mit mir führen?' Leahy, 'How dares the son of that man to
measure his renown with mine?' Rawl. B. 512 reads *Cid dobeir mac an
fir sin do comroma chucam-sa,* 'What brings the son of that man to stand
up to me?' (Meyer); Harl. 5280, *do comrama frium-sa*; H. 3. 18, *cid doberad*

a mac di comramh. Probably the lit. meaning is: 'What would bring his son to a combat against me?' i.e. 'Why should his son come?' Cf. chs. 12, 13. This interpretation is supported by ch. 16, '*Cid dano...chucci.*'

11. *do thairisem...do raind.* Cf. ch. 8. Thurneysen transl. 'Haltet den Wettstreit aufrecht'; Rawl. B. 512 and Harl. 5280, *in comroma do tairisim beus,* 'still keep up the contest' (Meyer). Cf. vocab. s.v. *tairissem.* I am inclined to think, however, that the phrase is an incomplete sentence, and merely repeats a part of the sentence (q.v. and note) in ch. 8 *ad fin.,* leaving the remaining half to be understood (*fagabar,* etc.); so also in some of the following chapters. The omission of *lécud* (cf. ch. 8 s.v.), however, is perhaps against this.

Atchonnarc-sa, with infixed pron. 3rd sing. masc. : 'I have seen him.' So MSS. Windisch suggested that this is for *atotchonnarc,* 'I have seen thee'; but such changes of person are common in this text. Meyer transl. 'I have seen him before.'

Cia...n-domḟacca, lit. 'which is the place in which thou hast seen me?' Cf. Windisch, *Gram.* § 218. Pedersen II, § 683 (3) note.

do thaige. Rawl. B. 512 adds *féin,* 'of your own house.' Thurneysen transl. 'Vor deinem Haus'; Leahy, 'It was before thine own house.'

Tanacaisiu...égim. Om. Rawl. B. 512, which reads: *Tarthusa mé gur' chaithis sleig form,* 'Thou metst me and castest a spear at me' (Meyer).

corra-ba...scíath. The exact force of *as* is uncertain. Thurneysen transl. 'dass er an meinem Schilde stak'; Leahy, 'and it was fixed in my shield,' i.e. (hanging) out of my shield. Meyer transl. 'so that it stood out of my shield.'

colluid, for *co-n luid,* 'so that it went.'

Atotchiat...súil, lit. 'The men of Ireland see you with one eye,' i.e. see that you are one-eyed. *atotchiat* (for *ad-dot-chiat*), 'they see thee,' with infixed pron. 2nd sing. Cf. vocab. s.v. *adcíu.*

in t-súil. The nom. is no doubt an error for the accus. as Windisch points out (cf. his Gloss. s.v. *súil* and note on p. 111 of *Irische Texte,* I). Harl. 5280 has the correct reading *in suil* (accus.). Windisch transl. 'Soll ich das andere Auge aus deinem Kopfe schlagen.' H. 3. 18 has *int suil n-aile.*

Dessid...dano. Rawl. B. 512 has *Ársin téit Oengus ina lebaid,* 'Then Oengus sat down on his couch' (Meyer).

12. *Frithalid...beus.* Rawl. B. 512 reads *In comroma beos, a Ulltu, ar Cet, no in muc do roind,* 'Still keep up the contest, men of Ulster,' saith Cet, 'or suffer me to divide the pig' (Meyer).

Nis-raindfe innossa. -*s*- is the infixed pron. 3rd sing. 'thou shalt not divide it.' Rawl. B. 512 has *ni roinnfir si bheos,* 'Thou shalt not divide it yet' (Meyer).

ar Cet. Rawl. B. 512 inserts *Is é, ar firu Er[enn],* 'It is he, say the men of Ireland' (Meyer).

Is...deóid. I think that the text is corrupt. The sentence appears to be

lit. 'It is I who have cleansed my falsehood at last' (? i.e. cleared myself
—my reputation—of the charge of falsely claiming the champion's right).
Thurneysen transl. 'Ich habe endlich Wort gehalten'; Leahy, 'I have but
one short word for thee.' But such an interpretation does not seem to me
possible. Can Thurneysen's 'Wort' be a misprint for 'Werth'? Rawl. B. 512
reads *mé roglan mo lám fádeóidh innat*, 'It was I that last cleaned my hands
in thee' (Meyer). H. 3. 18 has *mo goo fo deuidh i m-Muindremar*, 'it is I
who last cleaned my spears in M.,' which is probably correct. *gó, goo*
(for *gou*), 'spears,' acc. pl. Edd. have read *gó*, 'a lie,' and *a (Mun.)* as a voc.
instead of a prep.—which can hardly be right.

trí thráth. Windisch transl. *tráth*, 'Zeit, Stunde; die Namen der acht
canonischen Stunden'; Dottin, 'heure canonicale, moment'; Thurneysen
transl. our passage, 'Keine zwei Tage sind es her, dass ich,' etc.; Leahy,
'Not yet hath the third day passed since I,' etc.; Meyer, 'It is not three days
yet since I,' etc. Cf. ch. 3 note s.v.

im...chétmic, lit. 'around the head of your eldest son.'

Dessid...dano. Rawl. B. 512 has *Deisidh Muinremar ina śuide*, 'Munremar
sat down in his seat' (Meyer).

or Cet. Rawl. B. 512 inserts *no in muc do roind*, 'or I shall divide the pig'
(Meyer).

In comram beus. Cf. ch. 11 note s.v. *do thairisem*.

Rot-bia són. *-t-* is infixed pron. 2nd sing. 'that thou shalt have' (lit. 'that
shall be to thee').

Cid...chucum seems to be lit. 'What then...sons of boors with nicknames
at contest with me!' Thurneysen transl. 'Ei was! Der Sohn von Kerlen mit
Spitznamen kommt zum Wettstreit mit mir?' Meyer, 'What deem you that
the sons of churls with nicknames should come to contend with me?'

ar...sin. Rawl. B. 512 substitutes *Uáir bá misi bá sacart baistidh an anma
sin ar th' ath[air] si*, 'For it was I that was the priest who christened thy
father by that name' (Meyer). So also H. 3. 18 and Harl. 5280.

in t-ainm is the nom. of the article used for the accus.—a M. Ir. development. *Ainm* was originally neuter but became masc. with the disappearance
of the neuter about the tenth century.

.i. Cf. ch. 1 above, note s.v.

conna for *co-n na*, 'so that...not.'

oen-chois em.; LL. *oenchoss*. Rawl. B. 512 has *ænsal*, 'one heel.'

mac...chucum. Rawl. B. 512 reads *mac in f̣ir sin do chomroma cucum-sa*,
'What should bring the son of such a man to contend with me' (Meyer).

Dessid, etc. Rawl. B. 512 as above.

13. *In...beus.* Cf. ch. 11 note s.v. *do thairisem*.

mac Cuthechair. So LL. Cf. the inconsistency in spelling in the name of
Finn mac Cumall (originally Umall).

An bic. Cf. ch. 9 note s.v.

manip......chetóir. For *manip*, cf. ch. 3 note s.v., lit. 'unless it is for my (?)

crushing instantly.' Thurneysen transl. 'Nur langsam...wenn du mich nicht gleich zerquetschen willst'; Leahy, 'Pause thou a little...unless it be in thy mind to crush me in an instant.' For *fo chetóir* Rawl. B. 512 reads *ticce*. Meyer transl. 'Unless thou comest to pound me to pieces.' H. 3. 18 has *manip do imtuargain fo cetoir*, 'unless it be mutual slashing all at once.' This is no doubt the correct reading. LL. appears to have misread as *dom thuargain*.

da[no]. Rawl. B. 512 has *a cumma chaich*, 'like everyone else' (Meyer).

Dot-luid...dam-sa. Do-t-luid. This *t* is the infixed pron. 2nd sing. used normally ('There was a going to thee,' or 'it came to thee,' i.e. 'thou didst chance to be') as Thurneysen transl.: 'In einer Schlucht tratest du mir entgegen.' Windisch also seems to understand it so. Rawl. B. 512 has *co n-de-chais ar berna for ma chinn curteilcis gai form*, 'going into a gap before me thou didst throw a spear at me' (Meyer).

Atái...sin, lit. 'you are with disease of the urine from that time.'

no co, a variant of *ni-co(n)*, emphatic negative, 'not at all,' 'not.' Not to be confused with *no co*, 'until,' or with *nó co*, 'or that.' Cf. ch. 3 above s.v., and Dottin, *Manuel*, §§ 306, 401.

Cid dot-bérad. For *-bérad* see vocab. s.v. *dobiur*, lit. 'what would bring thee to me?' Cf. ch. 12.

14. *is...deilb*, lit. 'he is the making of a king in form.'

Ni buide frit, lit. '(There are) not thanks to thee.' Rawl. B. 512 reads *ni tuilli buidhe frit*, 'he earns no thanks from thee' (Meyer).

Cucainn...chét-gasciud. Thurneysen transl. 'Zu deinem ersten Waffengang zogst du gegen uns'; Leahy, 'It was against us that thou didst come on the day when thou didst first make trial of thy weapons.' H. 3. 18 reads *cucaindi cetatudchad-sai do chetgaiscced*; Harl. 5280, *cucainne ceta tudchadsa*; Rawl. B. 512, *cucaindi tucais-si do cetghaiscedh ar tús*, 'thou madest thy first raid to us' (Meyer).

conna...córai, lit. 'so that a word has not (been) found in correctness in your head,' or 'mouth.' Thurneysen: 'dass du kein Wort mehr richtig sprechen kannst'; Leahy, 'so that thou canst speak no word plainly.' Rawl. B. 512, *connách tic focal a córai tar do chend*, 'so that no word comes rightly over thy lips' (Meyer).

ro-loitt. Harl. 5280 reads *rotesc an gai fethe*. Meyer transl. 'sinews.'

conid...sin, lit. 'so that it is Cúscraid Mend which has chanced to you from that time.'

cóiced. Cf. ch. 5 note s.v.

15. *Rom-bertaigestar*. After *in tan* the verb is regularly nasalised. Cf. Thurneysen, *Gram.* § 491. Cf. vocab. s.v. *-bertaigestar* is deponent. Harl. 5280 has *rotmbertaicestar*; H. 3. 18, *rotmbertaigestair*; Rawl. B. 512, *rocer-taigh*, 'he made ready' (Meyer). The sentence may possibly mean 'he settled himself down in front of,' etc.

oc on muicc, i.e. *oc an muicc, an* the late form of the article (dat. sing. fem.).

co n-accatar. For this form cf. Pedersen II, § 683.

istech for *isa tech,* prep. *i(n)*+neut. accus. sing. of the article +accus. of *tech.* See note on *istaig* in ch. 6.

Ferait...Conall. Om. Harl. 5280; *in tan sin* adds Rawl. B. 512.

nod-mbertaigedar. Cf. ch. 4 s.v.; H. 3. 18, *nosmbertaigestor*; Harl. 5280, *nodbertaigedar.* It may be that hist. pres. and perf. forms have been confused by the scribes. The verb is no doubt an archaic one with which they were unfamiliar as a living form. Thurneysen transl. 'Conchobar selber nahm seinen Kopfschmuck vom Haupt und schwang ihn'; Leahy, 'Conor himself took his helmet from his head and swung it on high to greet him'; Rawl. B. 512 reads *Is and sin rolá Conchab[ar] a chathbarr día chend 7 nosber-taighend ina inadh feisin,* 'It was then Conchobar threw his helmet from his head and shook himself in his own place' (Meyer). The sentence is treated as a relative sentence after *is and,* hence the infixed -*dm*-, and cf. *Ériu,* vol. I, p. 162.

Is and, lit. 'It is then that.'

Is...thairiuc, i.e. 'It is good in our opinion our portion to be being prepared,' or more lit. 'our portion for preparing we consider good.'

lind. le is here used in the idiomatic sense 'in the opinion of'; *lind,* 'in our opinion.' Thurneysen, 'Ich bekäme gern meinen Antheil'; Leahy, ''Tis well that I wait for the portion that befalls me'; Rawl. B. 512 has *Is maith lind...ar cuit do tárr[acht]ain dún i n-erlaime,* 'We are pleased...that our portion is in readiness for us' (Meyer). *Cia rannas,* cf. Pedersen, II, § 520

Rod-dét...nod-ranna. Rod-dét is not common. H. 3. 18 and Harl. 5280 read *rodét.* Thurneysen transl. 'Es hat dem zugestanden werden müssen, den du dabei siehst'; Leahy, 'That office must be given to the man who stands there.' Rawl. B. 512 reads *Ruc óenfer d'feraib...ar comromaib a roind,* 'One man of the men of Ireland has obtained by contest the dividing of it.' *Rod-dét* is pret. pass. of *damaim,* 'I grant,' with infixed pron., as in *nod-ranna,* '(he) divides it,' *d* infixed pron. of 3rd sing.

nam-muicce. Cf. ch. 8 note s.v. *nam-mucci.*

londbruth loga. Cf. the same expression in the rhetorics in *Bricriu's Feast,* ch. 48.

gusfland ferge. Thurneysen takes this to mean blood ('zornwallendes Blut'); possibly 'heart.'

crechtaig cathbuadaig. I take these adjectives as gen. sing. limiting *curad,* with Windisch. Meyer translates differently,

> 'Red strength of anger under a hero's breast,
> Wound-inflicter, triumphant in battle, I see the son of Findchoem,'

which is not clear to me. Thurneysen takes *cathbuadaig* as a noun in apposition to *curad* and translates,

> 'Zornwallendes Blut in des Helden Brust,
> Des narbigen Schlachtensiegers!
> Du, sohn der Finnchaem, kannst dich mit mir messen.'

adcomsa. Harl. 5280 has the reading *atcoimsa*, not *atcoñsa* (as in Windisch). Rawl. B. 512, *atchim-si*, 'I see'; H. 3. 18, *atconn-sa*. The form of LL. has never been satisfactorily explained.

Conid. Cf. ch. 3 note s.v.

magen. Om. Meyer. Thurneysen transl. the phrase 'Ein Heldenort dein Herz von Eis'; Leahy, 'A dwelling-place for heroes thy heart of ice.' Meyer takes 'Heart of ice' and the phrases which follow as in apposition to Cet mac Matach. But cf. *maigne .i. mór,* O'Cl.; *maige,* 'great,' *Cath Catharda* (ed. Stokes, Leipzig, 1909).

cride n-ega. For the nasalisation cf. Dottin, *Manuel* § 58.

eithre n-ela, om. Rawl. B. 512. Poss. 'tail of a swan.'

tnúthach. Prob. 'anxious for fight ?' or 'jealous ?' Rawl. B. 512 has *cruthach,* 'shapely.'

Bid...im-chomruic-ni. So LL. Windisch adds : *ni ón ar Conall* with H. 3. 18 and Rawl. B. 512 : 'That will be...said Conall.' 'Verily it will be clear in our combat, said Conall' (Meyer). *bid...n-im-scarad.* Thurneysen transl. the whole passage,

> 'Das wird sich zeigen, wenn wir uns treffen,
> Und wird sich zeigen, wenn wir uns trennen.'

Leahy, 'That will be proved if we are in combat, that will be proved if we are separated.' Harl. 5280 reads *inarnimmcomracniu.*

bid airscela. Rawl. B. 512, *beitit arscela,* 'there will be stories.'

la Fer ṁ-brot. This may mean 'man of the goads,' 'oxen driver.' Rawl. B. 512, *la fer braitt.* But Meyer does not translate this or the following phrase.

Fer manath. H. 3. 18, *Fer mannach*; Rawl. B. 512, *fer manach. Fer ṁ-brot* and *Fer manath* are obscure. Om. Meyer and Windisch. Thurneysen transl.

> 'Der Ochsentreiber wird davon erzählen,
> Der Handarbeiter davon zeugen.'

Leahy,

> 'The goader of oxen (?) shall tell of it,
> The handcraftsman (?) shall testify of it.'

Adcichset...innocht. MSS. vary considerably in their readings here. Meyer does not attempt a translation. Harl. 5280 reads after *londgliaid*: *na da err eblaid echtair. acht regaid,* etc. Thurneysen transl. as follows:

> 'Helden werden zum wilden Löwen-kampf schreiten,
> Mann stürzt sich über Mann heut Nacht in diesem Haus.'

Leahy,

> 'Heroes shall stride to wild lion-strife,
> Man overturns man tonight in this house.'

H. 3. 18 has *arcichset,* probably a reduplicating fut. of a verb *arcing,* 'to march forward.' Pedersen (II, § 492) regards it as a corruption of *do-cichset,* from *do-cing.*

fer dar fer. I take the second *fer* to be sing. used for pl.; but it may be that *dar* is used in a more lit. and concrete sense ('the heroes will see...man (i.e. men) heaped on man,' etc.).

is taig. Cf. note in ch. 6.

16. *Cid...chucci*, i.e. 'What claim have you to take my place here' (viz. beside the pig)?

Is fir, lit. 'It is true,' or 'right,' i.e. 'you are entitled to,' etc. *Is* is possibly an error for *in*, 'Is it right?'

do chungid. I follow Windisch (cf. his Gloss. s.v. *cuingid*) in taking *do chungid* to be nom. sing. of verbal noun *cuingid* in apposition to *fir*, possibly 'It is verily so your seeking contest with me,' i.e. 'It is a fact that thou seekest,' etc. Cf. Thurneysen; Leahy, ''Tis true indeed...thou art contending in renown with me,' which does not give good sense. Rawl. B. 512 has *Is fír...do chuinccid comroma chucam-sa sin*, 'It is even so...that is to seek contest from me'; but we should probably read *In fír*, 'Can it be true?'

oen-chomram. I think that the word means a duel, 'single combat,' lit. 'single triumph,' 'single trophy.' Cf. Old Norse *Einvigi*. Cf. other compounds with *oen-*. Meyer transl. 'I shall give you contest'; Thurneysen, 'Ich will dir nur eines bieten.'

na toṅgat for earlier *a toiṅges*, with doubling of *an*, 'what,' *(a)n a(n)*. The pl. form of the verb is used with *tuath*. Cf. the phrase *toṅgu do día toiṅges mu thúath* (with rel. verb *toiṅges*, 'I swear by the god by whom my people swear,' Strachan, *Stories from the Táin* (text from *Yellow Book of Lecan*). Cf. vocab. s. v. *toṅgu.*

nach...aidchi. Thurneysen here accepts the text of Harl. 5280 (so also H. 3. 18, Rawl. B. 512), *nad raba cen goin duine cech oen* (om. Rawl. B. 512) *laithi do connochtaib ocus (gan* Rawl. B. 512) *orcain frid aighid* (om. Rawl. B. 512) *cech naidhci* (sic: *oenaidchi*, H. 3. 18, Rawl. B. 512) *ocus ni (noch* H. 3. 18) *ro codlus riam* (om. Rawl. B. 512) *cen cend connacht-[ach] fom glu[n]*, 'ist kein Tag vergangen ohne dass ich einen Connachter erschlagen habe, keine Nacht ohne Plünderung, und nie hab ich geschlafen ohne den Kopf eines Connachters unter meinem Knie'; 'I have never been a day without having slain a Connaughtman, or a night without plundering, nor have I ever slept without the head of a Connaughtman under my knee' (Meyer).

at...andó-sa. Cf. ch. 10 above, note s.v. *Is...andaisiu.*

is taig. Cf. ch. 6 note s.v.

ar araile. See Windisch, Gloss. s.v. *ar* (4). Thurneysen om. in his transl.; Leahy, 'in another fashion.' Rawl. B. 512 reads *f[or] araile.* Meyer transl. 'He would match thee contest for contest.'

nos-leice, lit. 'and he throws it.' For *nos leici...bruinni*, Harl. 5280 has *dolleci di Cet dar a brunne*; Rawl. B. 512, *7 léicidh co Cet dar a bruinde dó.*

cor-roimid...beolu. Leahy understands the blood to be Anlúan's and transl. 'and a gulp of the blood was dashed over his lips'; Meyer, 'so that a gush of blood broke over his lips'; Thurneysen, 'dass ihm ein Schluck Blut über die Lippen trat.' I think that the blood is Cet's own, caused to flow from his mouth by the violence of the blow on his chest. The point of the remark is to emphasise Conall's force.

cor-roimid, for *co-n-ro-memaid*. Cf. O'Connell, *Gram.* § 146.

17. *laech a thairismi*. Cf. ch. 8 note s.v. *tairismi*. Lit. 'a hero of its sustaining,' i.e. a hero capable of sustaining it; or 'a hero who will stand against him.' Cf. vocab. s.v. *tairissem*. Thurneysen transl. 'Doch fand sich unter den Connachtern kein Krieger ihn zu bestehen'; Leahy, 'But among the men of Connacht there was none who would challenge him.' Rawl. B. 512 reads ...*in tan sin laech a thairisme hi comromaib*, 'Truly there was not then found among the men of Connaught a warrior to stand up to him in contest' (Meyer). The same MS. adds, *ar roba lesc leo a marbad doráith*, 'for they were loath to be slain on the spot.'

imorro; bad patch in MS. Only *i* really clear and *m* fairly so.

damdabach, lit. 'an ox-vat.' Cf. Oıꝺe Cloınne Uıꞃnıᵹ (Soc. for the Preservation of the Ir. Lang.), ch. 29, where the three sons of Uisneach are said to have made a ꝺaınᵹeán of their shields around Deirdre, and she in the midst of them, when they leapt out over the ramparts of Emain among the hostile forces. The tactics appear to be the same.

ar...droch-daine. LL. reads *drochde*, but the MS. is not very clear here and Windisch's expansion is justified by the readings of the other MSS. Thurneysen transl. 'Denn im Haus begann die schlimme Sitte dass tückische Menschen hinterrücks Speere wurfen'; Leahy, 'For in that house was evil wrangling, and men in their malice would make cowardly casts at him.'

do...droch-daine. For *do chloendiburgun*, Harl. 5280 reads *do cloendibraicthib*, H. 3. 18, *di claondipractib*. Cf. vocab. s.v. *díburgun*; Rawl. B. 512, *ar doteilctis lu[cht] in leithi si na Clocha f[or] lu[cht] in leith aili*, 'for there was an evil custom in the house, the people of one side throwing stones at the people of the other side' (Meyer). I think that the passage has been misunderstood. The custom referred to is one analogous to, possibly connected with, the Scandinavian custom of bone-throwing (*knútu-kast*) at feasts, which we know to have been practised also in England. Cf. Saxo Grammaticus, *Dan. Hist.* transl. by O. Elton, p. 68; *Saxon Chronicle*, account of the death of Ælfheah (MS. Laud, ed. Plummer, *Two Saxon Chronicles*), s.a. 1012. The custom itself no doubt had its origin in the ordeal by which the valour of a champion was tested, as in our saga. Similar customs are said to exist among the aborigines of Australia. The incident in our saga is thus a regular part of the procedure, following naturally upon the verbal contest in which Conall had proved himself victor, and offering a further ordeal and test of courage. For *cloen* cf. Meyer, *Contributions*, s.v. (e.g. 'cross-eyed'). It is to be remembered however that *cloen*, 'squint-eyed,' is an epithet used in *Cath Ruis na Ríg*, ch. 56, of Conall Cernarch. *istaig*, 'indoors.' Cf. ch. 6 note s.v.

luid...de. Thurneysen transl. 'Nun machte sich Conall ans Zerlegen des Schweins; dazu nahm er das Ende des Schwanzes in den Mund. Und er sog den Schwanz, an dem neun Männer zu tragen hatten, ganz ein, dass er nichts davon übrig liess'; Leahy: 'And Conall turned to divide the Boar, and he took the end of the tail in his mouth. And although the tail was so great that it was a full load for nine men, yet he sucked it all into his mouth so that nothing of it was left.' Rawl. B. 512 reads after *dó roinn na muici*: *Rosúig in tarr uili 7 er nonb[air] bai ann, [con]nárfácaib banda de 7 rochuir a thuind 7 a srebhann úadh,* 'Then Conall went to divide the pig and took the end of its tail in his mouth until he had finished dividing the pig. He sucked up the whole tail, and a load for nine was in it, so that he did not leave a bit of it, and he cast its skin and membrane from him' (Meyer). Cf. note below.

cend in tarra. Previous edd. have taken *tarr* to be 'tail' here; but this does not seem to me to agree very well with *cor-ránic* or with what follows. Why should taking the tail between his teeth conduce to a division of the pig? And is not 'a load for nine men' a heavy weight for a pig's tail, even allowing for humorous exaggeration? I take it that Conall's feat is that instead of dividing the pig as a butcher and huntsman would and as was no doubt expected of him—lengthwise—he severed the hind-quarters from the fore-quarters by means of his teeth, having previously 'sucked in' the hind-quarters—a not inappropriate load for nine men—and leaving only the fore-quarters to the men of Connaught. This heroic feat would be quite in keeping with the tone of our story, and while Conall takes the lion's share he divides the pig according to the letter. It is to be noted however that in Mod. Ir. *tárr* means 'belly.'

cor-ránic dó. I take this to be lit. 'until it had come to him to divide,' i.e. until he finished dividing. Rawl. B. 512 reads *curuscáich dó roinn na muici,* 'until he had finished dividing the pig.'

nam-mucci. Cf. ch. 8 note s.v.

18. *thara[t]t.* I do not feel confident of this form. The vellum of LL. is bad at this point, and nothing is clearly visible after *thar.* Strictly speaking there is only room for one more letter, so possibly Rawl. B. 512, *thard,* is right; H. 3. 18 however reads *ni tarat,* which seems preferable, and Harl. 5280, *ni tharad.*

a da...brágid, lit. 'the two feet of the pig under the neck.' Rawl. B. 512, *cethraime na muici [nó] da cois na muici fo braghait,* 'a quarter of the pig, or the two fore-legs of the pig' (Meyer).

cor-riacht, for *co-n+riacht* (serves as *t*-pret. of *riccim,* 'I reach,' from *ro+síacht*), 'until,' or 'so that he came to,' 'reached.' The sentence lit. is 'and each reached at the other,' i.e. 'made a grab at.'

dar ó i suidiu. So also H. 3. 18; Thurneysen, 'Da gab es Backenstreiche'; Leahy, 'They buffeted each other'; Rawl. B. 512 reads *tar cluáis 7 tar cend and sin,* 'Then there were blows over ear and head'; Harl. 5280, *darho hi suidi;* H. 3. 18, *dar a ó i suidiu.* For *i suidiu* cf. Pedersen II, § 514 (9).

in carnail...taigi. Rawl. B. 512, *in carn do corpaib na laech robái for a lár,* 'so that the heap of the warriors' bodies on the floor was as high as the side of the house' (Meyer).

ro-bái. Fo appears in LL. for *ro,* no doubt a scribal error.

co...dorsi. Rawl. B. 512, *Ar romarbtha ceith[ri] c[ét]* 7 *míli fer n-armach it[er] Ulltu* 7 *Conn[acht]a andsin, corom[a]idhet[ur]* [*secht*] *srotha do fuil* 7 *do chrú amach dar na secht n-doirrsib,* 'For there were slain one thousand and four hundred armed men both of Ulster and Connaught, so that seven streams of blood and gore burst through the seven doors' (Meyer).

co suifed fuil mol. Uncertain. *co ralsat soimal for lar an tigi no an lis,* Harl. 5280; *coralsat for lar ind lis,* H. 3. 18. Thurneysen transl. 'Und gewaltiges Getöse erhob sich. Das Blut auf dem Boden des Gehöftes hätte eine Mühle drehen können, so hieb einer auf den andern ein'; Leahy, 'And great was the din that uprose; the blood upon the floor of the house might have driven a mill, so mightily did each man strike out at his fellow.' Rawl. B. 512, *curolásat gáir mór for lár ind lis,* 'and raised a great shout in the middle of the close.' Thurneysen's translation is indirectly supported by MS. Ed. XXXVI (see p. 55 below). *suifed,* 3rd sing. cond. of *sói,* 'to turn.'

liss. Cf. ch. 5 note s.v.

Is...fremaib. The force of *dóib* is made clearer in the reading of MS. Ed. XXXVI (cf. p. 55 below). I take it, with Thurneysen, to refer to Fergus's enemies. 'Damals riss Fergus eine grosse Eiche aus den Wurzeln, die mitten im Gehöfte stand, und schwang sie gegen die andern.' Leahy om.

dóib. Gabaim with *do,* 'to occupy oneself with something,' 'to attend to something vigorously.' Fergus laid about him. Rawl. B. 512 expands the passage considerably: *Is and sin gabais Ferg[us] dóib .i. do Con[n]achtaib in n-daraig móir bái f[or] lár ind liss iarna beím dó asa fremaib. Atberat araili is é Curí mac Dáiri rogab in n-daraig dóib,* 7 *is ann sin doriacht s[o]m íat, ar ni raibi nech d'feraib M[u]man and reimhe sin, acht Lug[aid] m[a]c Conrí* 7 *ceteri pauci. O doríacht Curíi íat, ruc leth na muici [con]a d[ru]i[m] ó Leith Cuinn a oenar. Maidid tra díb asin lis amach. Dogníat cath i n-dorus an lis beos,* 'Then Fergus took the great oak that was in the middle of the close to the men of Connaught, after having torn it from its roots. Others say that it was Curói mac Dári who took the oak to them, and it was then that he came to them, for there was no man of Munster there before, except Lugaid, son of Curói, and a few others. When Curói had come to them, he carried off alone one half of the pig with its back from Leth Cuinn. Then they broke forth from the close into the field. They continue to fight in front of the close.'

Doberar...liss, or perhaps 'The combat took place in the door of the *liss.*' Thurneysen transl. *maidit...liss,* 'Dann stürzten sie aus dem Gehöfte hinaus, und der Kampf ging draussen weiter'; Leahy, 'and they all burst out of the court, and the battle went on outside.' Rawl. B. 512 reads *Maidid tra díb asin lis amach. Dogníat cath i n-dor[us] on lis beos,* 'Then they broke forth from the close into the field. They continue to fight in front of the close' (Meyer). For the word *less*, cf. ch. 5 note s.v.

19. *co ro-leiced*, lit. 'so that it was let loose.' Rawl. B. 512 reads *curoleíc*; Harl. 5280, *corailcet*; H. 3. 18, *corrailced*.

no-thogad, a late form of the 3 sing. condit. The readings of Harl. 5280 and H. 3. 18 preserve the earlier form *dongegadh*, 3rd sing. conditional.

rús con. H. 3. 18 has *rustogh. rús*, from *ro-fíus*, 'great knowledge.' Cf. *dús* (from *do-fíus*) above.

ocus ro-leci...Connachta. Thurneysen, 'Und stürzte sich auf die erliegenden Connachter; denn diese flohen.' Leahy, 'And the hound joined himself with the men of Ulster, and he rushed on the defeated Connaughtmen, for these were in flight.' If *ro-leci* is intrans. we may transl. 'he set himself to slay the Connaughtmen who had been defeated.' It is more probable, however, that the subject of *ro-leci* is Mac Dathó. Cf. the reading of Rawl. B. 512, *gurleic Mac Dátho in coin ina díaid* (*ro-leci*, trans.). Rawl. B. 512 adds 7 *f[or]fób[air] for letrad Connacht co mór*, 'and (the hound) set to tearing the men of Connaught greatly.'

Asberat-som. Before this Rawl. B. 512 inserts *Dochóidh Ai[li]ll 7 Medb ina carpat 7 a n-ara leo gurléic M[a]c Dátho in coin ina n-díaid*, 'Ailill and Medb went into their chariot, and their charioteer with them, and Mac Dathó let the hound after them' (Meyer).

donáraill. Thurneysen transl. 'Da traf ihn Fer-Loga, der Wagenlenker von Ailill und Medb, so, dass sein Rumpf auf die Seite fiel'; Leahy, 'and there Ferloga, charioteer of Ailill and Maev, fell upon him, so that he cast his body to one side'; Rawl. B. 512, *Is and sin dorat ara Ai[le]lla 7 Medba builli don choin curolá a coland for leith*, 'Then the charioteer of Ailill and Medb dealt the hound a blow so that he sent its body aside; and that,' etc. (Meyer). The word *donáraill* (cf. vocab. s.v.) only appears to occur here and in the *Félire Oengus*. It is 3rd sing. pret. of *to-ad-ell* (from *ell-*, 'to go,' with infixed pron. 3rd sing. masc.+*ro*). See Pedersen, II, § 711.

in charpait. Rawl. B. 512 adds *oc Ibhar Cinn [Chonn], un[de] [Connacht]a d[icu]nt, 7 asberat s[o]m di[diu] is ón coin sin rohainmnigthea Muighi Ailbe, úair rob Áilbe ainm in chon*, 'at Ibar Cinn Chon (the Yew-tree of the Hound's Head), whence Connaught takes its name' (Meyer).

20. *Dolluid.* Cf. vocab. s.v. *dollod* and cf. ch. 13 note s.v. *dot-luid.*

Beluch, etc. The modern equivalents of the names which follow, so far as they can be identified, are entered in the index of proper names at the end of the book (see p. 71 ff. below). I have accepted O'Donovan's and O'Curry's identifications (*Lectures on the MS. Material of Ancient Ireland*, p. 487) where sanctioned by Hogan. Cf. also K. Meyer, ed. cit. p. 64. It will be noted that the list of names forms a tiny *Dindsenchas* for Co. Kildare and perhaps beyond, and may be compared to the journey of the Twrch Trwyth in Kilhwch and Olwen, cf. Introduction, p. 8 above. For *for Áth M.* Rawl. B. 512 reads *sech,* 'past.'

fris rater, lit. 'to which is said,' a regular idiom in stating proper names.

mac Lugnai. H. 3. 18 and Rawl. B. 512 read *mic Lugna*, 'of the sons of Lug.'

ro-lá appears to be used intransitively, as elsewhere in the saga, cf. ch. 3. It is not impossible however that Ferloga is the subject.

donarlaic. Cf. vocab. s.v. *tar-laicim*. Windisch, 'er liess sich herab auf die Heide' (cf. his Gloss. s.v.).

Beir buide n-anacuil, i.e. 'Give a reward for (your) deliverance.' MSS. vary considerably here. Harl. 5280 reads *emd*; H. 3. 18, *einn*, Rawl. B. 512 *Indarlem nocha...raghthar de*, 'Methinks thou wilt not get hence' (Meyer). For this passage, and for *cepóc*, see Zimmer, *Kelt. Stud.* I, p. 34 ff.

T'óg-ríar, lit. 'your complete satisfaction'; Rawl. B. 512 has *t'uagreir* (acc.) *deit*, which Meyer transl. : 'thy full will to thee,' i.e. have thy wish.

cepoc. I believe this to be an extempore panegyric. Cf. O'Curry, *On the Manners and Customs of Ancient Ireland*, vol. III, p. 371. We may cf. the *slava* or choral panegyric which was performed over Russian heroes at the medieval court of Kiev. From the *Slovo* or 'Word of Igor's Armament' (cf. transl. L. A. Magnus, London, 1915) we learn that such a panegyric chorus was also sung by women, especially on the return of a hero after a heroic feat. O'Curry, *loc. cit.*, quotes a couplet from a gloss in 'an ancient vellum MS.':

'The praise of the king of Loch
Is (a) better (subject) for our cepóc.'

cech nóna. So Windisch and Meyer; 'jede neunte Stunde' (Thurneysen); 'at each ninth hour' (Leahy).

Ba écen ón, lit. 'That was necessary'; Rawl. B. 512, *rotfía són ar Conch[obar]*, 'Thou shalt have that,' said Conchobar.

ar...Conchobar. The use of *chena* here is uncommon; but Meyer compares LL. 103 a *ní étaim-sea chena*, 'I cannot do otherwise' (cf. *Contributions*, s.v. *cen* 2). Thurneysen, 'Denn man wagte es nicht zu verweigern, Conchobars wegen'; Leahy, 'for they dared not to deny him, fearing the wrath of Conchobar'; Rawl. B. 512, *Ba heicen di[diu] do ingenaib Emna sin do dénam, ar ní lamhdaíss cena lá Conch[obar] gen a dénam*, 'That the maidens of Emain Macha had to do, for they did not dare to do otherwise for (fear of) Conchobar.' *Chena* appears to be used in its original sense, 'without it' (E. Ir. *cenae, cene + é*), i.e. 'they did not dare without doing it,' 'they did not dare not to do it.' H. 3. 18 has *ar ni lamdis cena denam*.

ra-leiced. Thurneysen, 'wurde Ferloga über die Luan-Furt nach Connaught entlassen'; Leahy, 'and at the end of a year Ferloga crossed,' etc. Rawl. B. 512 reads *roléic* and om. *Ferloga*, 'he (i.e. Conchobar) let him (i.e *Ferloga*) go back to the West to Athlone.' Rawl. B. 512 adds *7 ní ruc na cepóca cé ruc na heocha. Conidh hé sin scaradh Ul[ad] oc[us] Connacht im choin M[i]c Dáthó 7 immá muic*, 'But he did not get the *cepóca*, though he got the horses. And this is how Ulster and Connaught fell out about the hound of Mac Dáthó and about his pig.'

ADDITIONAL NOTE ON MS. EDINBURGH XXXVI.

It has been mentioned in the Introduction (cf. pp. 2 ff. above) that MSS. LL., Harl. 5280, H. 3. 18 and Rawl. B. 512 offer substantially identical versions of our saga. With the exception of a single passage in Rawl. B. 512, ch. 18, which indicates a variant tradition, the differences in narrative between these MS. versions are merely verbal. Rawl. B. 512 however offers some variation in the poems quoted, and in the order of the contests (chs. 9—15). The Edinburgh text of the Saga, on the other hand (MS. Edinburgh XXXVI) shows much wider divergence from the other versions than do any of these from one another. These differences may be briefly summed up as (1) verbal, (2) differences in narrative, (3) differences in the poems quoted.

As examples of (1) we may refer to the passage (ch. 15) in which the description of Conchobar's joy on seeing Conall Cernach entering is described as follows: *Is ansin do cuir Conqbar a chathbarra cuana clochorrdha caomhbhuadhach da chen. Do chuir fiorchaon failte fria Conall Cerrnach.*

The *cepóc* demanded by Ferloga in the Irish versions (ch. 19) is referred to in Ed. XXXVI as a *cepog* and a *duthchan.*

The arrival of the rival cavalcades from Ulster and Connaught (ch. 5) is pictured slightly differently. *Do riachtadur an da choigeadh is ferr bhadur an Eirinn go rabatur an dorus bruighne Mic Da Shogh. Tuirling an marctshluagh ar gach taobh don bruighin and ba furachur fri gach a ccoimhed ar a cheile* etc.

The hero is generally called Mac Da Shogh. Bricriu's name (ch. 6) is given as *Breicin mac Cairbre Chinnleith,* and in ch. 7, *Senlaech Arad* of LL. appears as *sen laoch amhra o Cruachan Conacht anoir; Cruachniu... Conalad* as *Cruinne mac Cruaithlinn Connacht; In Loth mór* as *Iarloit* (cf. Rawl.); Mac Dathó's offer to the Ulster messengers is somewhat expanded (ch. 4) and Conall's division of the pig is described (ch. 17) with slightly variant details.

(2) More significant than verbal details are (2) the expansions and omissions in the incidents of the narrative. Again to quote a few examples only:

After the offers of the Connaught and Ulster messengers have been received by Mac Dathó (ch. 2), the former add a further speech in Ed. XXXVI, summing up the situation as it appears to them. *'Dar ar briatribh,'* ar techta Conacht, *'bu dorcha ce & cabhan & bó bronach tuaith & taoisigh & treabhadh coigidh Laigen uile da diultadh Medb & Oillil fan ccoin.'*

A prose dialogue is quoted between Conall Cernach and Cet Mac Matach (ch. 15) before the dialogue poem. It no doubt takes the place of the brief altercation between them which in LL. etc. occurs at the beginning of ch. 16, but in the Edinburgh text it is fuller.

Some picturesque details are inserted (ch. 17) with regard to Conall's eating the pig's tail or hind quarters : *Is ansin ro gabh Conall cen tarra na muic na bheol, gur shuigh chuige i ionnus go meileadh rioghmhullion ar gach sroth saille ro bhui ag silleadh ar gach taobh dia bheol.* Other MSS. have perhaps retained a corrupt reminiscence of this phrase, but in a different connection (cf. ch. 18, note s.v. *co suifed fuil mol* above).

The narrative of the fight within the house (ch. 18) is considerably expanded, by a vivid account of clod and clay throwing and 'sodding.' The account of the combat in the *liss* is also fuller, and that of Fergus's exploit, while it offers no fresh incident, is a much fuller and more intelligible account than the brief sentence in LL. It mentions, e.g., that Fergus was unarmed, and thus gives a raison d'être for his plucking a *craobh dharach* or oaken stave with which to lay about him. It also makes clear that his animosity was directed against the men of Connaught.

In Ed. XXXVI the contests with Eogan mac Durthacht and Oengus mac Láma Gábaid are omitted. Details which in the Irish MSS. occur in the narrative of the former appear in Ed. in connection with the contest with Cúscraid Mend Macha, which is thus somewhat expanded. In the account of the contest with Loegaire Buadach occur the remaining details of the contest attributed in the Irish texts to Eogan mac Durthacht. Loegaire's contest also is thus considerably expanded. Place-names are also added to this contest in Ed. which do not occur in any of the Irish contests ; and I suspect traces here also of the contest attributed elsewhere to Oengus mac Láma Gábaid (*do theithadh umam ar gach taobh and do lenus me sech cach and do theilgis do thshleigh foram and do theilgus an tsleigh cedna fort no go ndeçhuidh tɪ id*).

On the other hand, the omissions in the Edinburgh text are equally significant. Thus whereas in the Irish versions seven Ulster heroes challenge Cet before the appearance of Conall Cernach, in the Edinburgh text only five such champions' challenges are retailed, those of Eogan mac Durthacht and Oengus mac Láma Gábaid being omitted, as we have seen.

The incident of the *damdabach*, the *drochduine, drochcostud* and *cloendiburgun*, and Conall's danger while dividing the pig, which occur in all the Irish versions (ch. 17), are wholly omitted.

Of the little '*dindsenchas*' (ch. 20), which also occurs with little variation in all the Irish versions, the Scottish version has no trace. The only place-names mentioned are Ath Chin Chon and Mag Ailbe.

(3) The most important difference however is in ch. 15, where the dialogue poem between Cet and Conall, which occurs in all the Irish versions, is omitted. Its place is taken by a dialogue poem wholly different in substance, form and metre.

'A Chonall chaoimh chomhramhuidh / a laoich leidmigh leadairthigh
   a fir choimhed an chuigidsa / na ben don mhuic mor-adhbuilsi,
Is misi an curaidh curaidhlaidir / chenglus tu go curannta,
   churaidh chaomh na Craobhruaidh(e) / a fiaghnu(i)s chaomh
                             Chonchubar,

Eirigh, a Ched chomramhuidh/on mhuic mhaisi mor-adhbhuilsi
is leig a roin go rothapaidh/do Chonchubar is da churadaibh.
Na gabh-sa dian-comurle/o curadhuibh na Cruachan-sa
techt do chosnamh curaidmhire/re hairachtuibh Emhna fheruaine.

While differing substantially from all the Irish versions the Edinburgh
MS. is closer to Rawl. B. 512 than to the other three. This affinity is not
particularly striking in the substance of the narrative in which, as we have
seen, Rawl. is generally in close agreement with the other Irish texts. It
is, however, worth noting that in the order of the contests Rawl. and Edin.
are identical, but differ from the other versions.

The verbal correspondence is even more striking. To quote a few examples
only: in ch. 1 Rawl. and Edin. read 'This was the fifth *bruiden*' etc. where
the other texts have 'sixth,' and both omit the *bruiden* of Blai Briuga from
the list which follows. Both specify that the *bruiden* of Forgall Manach was
'at Lusk.' Both state in ch. 1 that the hound Ailbe ran round the whole of
Leinster in one day—statements not found in this form in the other texts.

In the last chapter both add the information—not found in the other
texts—that though Ferloga got the horses he did not get the *cepóc*.

More important is the fact that in chs. 1, 17 both Rawl. and Ed. quote
identical fragments of two poems not contained in any of the other texts,
while both omit the poem in ch. 3 which all the other texts quote.

VOCABULARY

(The numbers refer to the Chapters of the Text. Aspirated forms are usually given without aspiration.)

A.

a, voc. particle (aspirating)

-a-, infixed personal pronoun, 3 sg. m., n.

a, poss. pron. m. and n. 3 sg. (aspirating) 'his,' 'its'; fem. 3 sg. geminating 'her'; pl. (nasalising), 'their.' The *n* of the nasalisation is written before vowels and before *b*, *d*, *g*; is assimilated to a following *l*, *m*, *n*, *r*; is not written before *c*, *t*, *f*, *s*

-an-, infixed personal pronoun, 3 sg. m., n.

a, an, neuter of the article, cf. *in*, *ind*

a, an, relative pronoun (often written *i*, *in*) 'which,' 'who.' The original initial *s*, generally lost, remains after the preps. *co (cussa n-), for (forsa n-), fri (frissa n-, rissa n-), le (lassa n-).* This word is ident. w. the neuter form of the article used relatively

a, ass, prep. w. dat. 'from,' 'out of'; frequently combined w. the art., e.g. *assind* 10, and with prons., e.g. *assa* 16, 18

a, prep. Cf. *fo*

acaib, cf. *oc*

accallaim, 'I converse,' 'talk,' pres. sg. 1 deponent subj. *an bic...co rot-acilliur* 'wait a little so that I may speak to you' 9

accatar, cf. *adcíu*

acht, 'but,' 'except,' 'only' 3, 6, 12 etc.; For 3 see note s.v. *acht co*

acilliur, cf. *accallaim*

acus, 'and,' cf. *ocus*

adbar, m. 'material' 14, cf. *adbhar sagairt* 'a clerical student'

adcíu, v. 'I see'; *atchi* 2 sg. (for *ad-d-chi*) 'thou seest it,' with infixed pron. 3 sg. n. 9; The form *atotchiat* 3 pl. (for *ad-dot-chiat*) 'they see you,' contains a pronoun of the second person 11; for *adcichset*, redupl. s-fut. 3 pl. 15 see note; *facca* perf. 2 sg. *cia airm i n-dom-facca* 'where have you seen me?' 11; *accatar* 3 pl. (*co n-accatar*) 15

adcomsa 15. See note ad loc.

áel, m. 'a flesh-fork,' acc. *in n-ael* 1

áen, 'one,' cf. *óen*

aere, 'burden' 17

ag, n. 'cow,' 'deer' 7; n. pl. *aige* 6

ágach, 'warlike' 15

aidche, f. 'night' 16

aig, f. 'ice'; sing. gen. *ega* 15

aige, cf. *ag*

aiged, f. 'face'; pl. n. *aigthe carat* 'faces of friends' 5

aigedaib, cf. *óege*

ail, f. 'insult,' 'disgrace'; sg. acc. 14

aile, sg. m., f.; *aill* n. 'other' 5; gen. *aile* 3; nom. for acc. *aile* 11; *n-aill* 13

ainm, n. 'name' 19; pl. d. *cusna les-anmannaib* 12, *les-ainm* 'a nickname' 12

aire, m.; nom. pl. *airig* 'chief'

airec (verb n.), 'finding,' 'waiting for.' Cf. *tairec* 'attending upon.' Dat. *do airiuc thuile doib* 'um ihr Begehren entgegen zu nehmen?' (Windisch) 2

airiuc, cf. *airec*

airle, f. 'counsel' 3

airm, f. 'place' 11

airscele, *airscela* 'famous story,' 'report of a warrior's prowess,' 'reputation' 15

ais, 'the back.' *dar aiss*, lit. 'across or over the back,' 'behind' 20

aithesc, n. 'intimation,' 'statement,' 'message'; dat. sing. *athesc* 4; pl. acc. *aithescae* 2, H. 3, 18, *athiusca* Harl. 5280

all, n. 'bridle'; pl. dat. *co n-allaib* 20

ám, 'indeed' 10

amlaid, 'thus' 14

am-maidm, cf. *maidm*

amne, 'thus' 6 Harl. 5280

amra, 'wonderful,' 'marvellous' 1; also n. 'a wonder,' 'marvel'

an, cf. *anaim*

anacul, 'deliverance,' 'escape'; sg. gen. *anacuil* 20

anaim, 'I remain,' 'wait,' pl. 3 *anait* 4; imper. sg. 2 *an* 9, 13; pret. sg. 3 *an* (e.g. *co ro-an*) 19

anair, 'from the east' 5

and, prep. + pron. 3 sg. 'there,' 'then,' 'in it'; combined with the demonstr. *sin, andsin, andso* etc., cf. s.v. *fecht*

anda, adas, andat, andó, cf. *-táu*

andaisiu, 10, cf. *-táu* and note

andes, 'from the south' 20

andso, cf. *and*

ane, 'then,' 'therefore' (Meyer); Windisch suggests emendation to *amne* 6, 12

aníar, 'from the west' 5, 7

anim, f. 'blemish,' 'defect' 16

anúas, 'from above' 6

apa, 'cause'; *ar apaide* 'however' 5

ar, prep. w. dat. and acc. 'on account of,' 'because of,' 'on the grounds of,' 'for.' *ar araile* 'in addition to' 16 (Windisch); *ar chena* 'in addition to' 6 etc.; *ar mug* 'to a slave' 3; *ar ar m-belaibni* 'before our faces' 9; *ar mo chind-sa* 13; *ar deilb* 14; with suffixed pron. 3rd sg. fem. acc. *aire* 3? Freq. confused w. *for*

ar, 'since,' 'for' 12, 14

ar, 'said he (she)' 2, 4, 6; also written *or, ol*

ár, n. 'massacre' 5, 19

ar, pron. poss. pl. 1 (nasalising), 'our'; combined w. preps. *inar* 15, *ar ar* 9

ara, m. 'charioteer' 20

araile, 'the other'; acc. *co araile* 3, *ar araile* 16

ard, 'high,' 'great'

arg, m. 'hero'; pl. nom. *airg,* 15?

ar-raind, cf. *rannaim*

as, prep. 'out of,' 'from'

asbiur, 'I say,' pres. indicative pl. 3 *asberat* 19, pret. sg. 3 *asbert* 3, 15. W. infixed particle *a-t-biur,* 'I say,' sg. 3 *atbeir*; pl. 3 *atberat* 19, imperf. sg. 2 *atbertha-su* 3, pret. sg. 3 *atbert* 15

ascad, 'gift,' 'present,' pl. acc. *ascada* 4

asóim, 'I turn away from'? sg. 3 *asoí* 3

ata-nebla, perhaps for *ad-don-ebla,* 'he will drive (?crush) us'? 3

atáu, 'I am,' sg. 2 *atái* 13, 3 *atá* 3, 16, 19; pl. 3 *atát* 6. Cf. *-táu*

atbertha, cf. *asbiur*

atchí, cf. *adcíu*

at-chomnaic (perfect), 'It happened'; with infixed pron. sg. 2 *atotchomnaic* lit. 'has fallen upon thee,' i.e. 'thou hast been' 14

at-chonnarc (perfect, for *at-chondarc,* with infixed pron. 3 sg. masc.), 'I saw him,' 'caught sight of him' 11

atesta, cf. *tess-tá*

áth, m. 'a ford'; sg. dat. *áth* 20

athair, m. 'father' 12

athenim, 'I entrust,' 'commit,' 'commend,' pass. pres. sg. 3 *athenar*

athesc, cf. *aithesc*

atotchiat, cf. *adcíu*

atotchomnaic, cf. *at-chomnaic*

atracht, cf. *atraig*

atraig, 'he raises himself,' pres. pl. 3 *atragat* 18; t-pret. sg. 3 *atracht* 4

atlúi, 'he escapes'; 2 sing. pret. *atrullais fein* 9

au, ó, m. 'ear,' *ó* 18

aurdarcus, m. 'fame,' 'renown,' 'distinction,' sg. dat. *aurdarcus* 1

B.

ba, cf. *is.* For *ro-bá* cf. *-táu*

bachlach, m. 'herdsman,' 'rustic,' 'boor' 12

bad, cf. *is*

badb, a war goddess

baile, bale, m. 'place'; *bale* with the prep. *i n-* and a following relative sentence 'a place where,' e.g. *bale itaat* 6

báire, 'the goal,' 'the game of hurling' 9

bar, poss. pron. pl. 2; used in M.Ir. for the infixed pron.

bas, cf. *is*

batar, cf. *-táu*

bec, becc, 'little,' 'small' 18; instr. used adverbially *bic* 9

béim, n. 'striking,' verbal n. of *benim* 'I strike'; sg. dat. *do béim* 7

bél, m. 'a lip'; pl. dat. *bélaib* 9, 10, acc. *beolu* 16

ben, f. 'woman' 3; in compos. *ban-*; gen. *mná* 3, dat. *mnái,* acc. *mnái,* pl. dat. *mnáib* 3

benaim, benim, 'I strike'; pret. sg. 3 *co m-ben* 10

bered, cf. *berim*

berim, 'I bear,' 'bring,'; imper. *beir* 20; imperf. sg. 3 *bered* 1; t-pret. sg. 3 *co m-bert,* t-fut. pl. 3 *bertait* 4; pass. fut. sg. 3 *berthair* 3; verb. n. *breith* 20

berna, f. 'breach,' 'gap,' dat. sg. *i mbernai* 13

bertaigim, 'I shake,' 'brandish,' 'flourish'; pres. dep. sg. 3 *rom-* (?nom-) *bertaigedar* 4, *rod-* (?nod-) *mbertaigedar* 15; s-pret. dep. sg. 3 *rom-bertaigestar* 15

berthair, cf. *berim*

bés, m. 'custom' 9

béus, 'further,' 'yet again' 11 ff.

biad, n. 'food' 3, 4, 6

biaid, cf. *-táu*

biathaim, 'I nourish'; pass. imperf. sg. 3 *no-biata* 5, infin. acc. *biathad* 5 bic, cf. *bec*

bid, cf. *is*

bith, cf. *-táu*

bláith, 'smooth,' 'gentle'; sg. dat. *bláith*

bliadain, f. 'year'; gen. *bliadna* 2, gen. pl. *blia[dan]* 5; *dia bliadna* 'that day a year hence' 20

bó, f. 'cow'; pl. gen. *bó*, dat. *buaib* 3

boccóit, 'buckler,' 'shield,' 'boss'; dat. pl. *boccótib* 17

boí, 'was'; pret. sing. 3 of the substantive verb. Cf. *-táu*

bráge, 'neck'; gen. *bráget* 14; dat. *brágid* 18; acc. *brágit* 14

brat, m. 'cloak'

bráthair, m. 'brother' 7

breith, cf. *berim*

bríathar, f. 'word'

bríg, f. 'power,' 'force,' 'strength,' 'might'

briugu, m. 'husbandman' 1

bruden f. 'court,' 'palace' (Windisch); 'hostel,' 'banqueting hall,' K. Meyer. Cf. note s.v.

bruinne, m. 'breast'; acc. *bruinni* 16

bruth, n. 'glowing metal,' 'red-hot metal' 15

buadach, 'victorious'; in compos. cf. *cathbuadaig* 15

buaib, cf. *bó*.

budech, 'thankful,' 'grateful,' 'satisfied,' 'pleased'; pl. nom. *buidig* 4

buide, 'thanks,' 'satisfaction,' 'reward' 14; acc. *buide* 20

buidig, cf. *budech*

buile, buille, builli, f. 'a blow,' 'stroke'; sg. acc. *buille* 6; pl. nom. *builli* 18

C.

cach, cech, adj. 'each,' 'every'; f. acc. *cech* 20; dat. *cach* 1; dual acc. *cech* 5

cách, pron. 'everybody,' 'the others' 10 etc.

cáin, 'choice,' 'excellent,' 'beautiful' 15

cangen, f. 'business,' 'affair,' 'contract,' 'trouble'; sg. dat., e.g. *tria changin*

cara, m. 'friend'; sg. dat. *do charait* 2; pl. gen. *carat* 5

caratrad, 'friendship' 2

carnáil, f. 'a heaping,' 'piling up'; 'a heap,' 'pile' 18

carpat, m. 'a chariot'; gen. *carpait* 19, dat. *carput* 20, acc. *carpat* 9

cath, m. 'battle' 3

cathbúadach, gen. *-aig* 'victorious in battle' 15

cech, cf. *cach*

céle, m. 'a mate'; gen. *ceile* 6; dat. *ceiliu* 3

cen, prep. w. acc. 'without' 2, 3

cena, chena, 'without it,' 'otherwise' 20, *ar chena* 6, 'moreover,' 'besides'

cend, m. 'head,' 'end,' 'chief' 19; gen. *chind* 16, dat. *cind, ciund, cend, dia chind* 'from his head' 15; *ar cend* 'towards,' 'for' 4; *co cend* 'until the end' 5; *i cind bliadna* 'at the end of a year' 2

cen-motha, 'besides,' 'in addition to' 2, 6

cennide, 'headgear,' 15

cepóc, f. 'panegyric.' Cf. note s.v. 20

cert, adj. 'right,' 'just'; noun 'right,' 'justice'

cét, 'hundred' 2, 5 (pl. n.)

cét-, 'the first' (only found as the first element of a compound) 1, 12, 14

cétna, 'the first,' 'the same,' 1, 2, 10, 11; used adverbially 'first' 14

cétumus, 'in the first place,' 11

charait, cf. *cara*

chét, cf. *cét-*

chétóir, cf. *ór*

chom-máin, cf. *com-máin*

chon, cf. *cú*

chotlod, cf. *cotlud*

chotulta, cf. *cotlud*

chuci-sium, cf. *co, -som*

chucut-su, cf. *co, -su*

chungid, cf. *cuingid*

cía, interrog. indecl. pron. 'who,' 'whoever,' 'what' 11, 12 etc.

cia, conj. 'although'

cích, f. 'breast'; dat. sing. *cich* 15

cid, interrog. pron. 'what' 10 etc.

cid, *ce* + 3 sg. subj. of copula, 'though 3?

cin, m. 'guilt,' 'offence,' 'fault,' 'crime'

cind, cf. *cend*

cinnas (from *ce indas*), 'how,' 'what kind' 6, 7

claideb, m. 'sword'; gen. *chlaidib*, dat. *claidiub* 12

clóen, 'cross-,' 'evil,' 'wrong,' 'perverse'; in cpds. *do cloendiburgun* 17

co, prep. w. acc. 'to,' 'unto,' 'till'; w. pers. prons. sg. 1 *chucum* 12, 2 *chucut-su* 13, 3 m. *chuci*, f. *chucci*; pl. 1 *cucain-ni* (with additional suffixed pron.) 9, 3 *chucu*; with possessive prons. sg. 3 *co a* 3, 5; used with the adjective to form adverbs

co, co n-, prep. w. dat. 'with' 3, 11; in conjunction w. the article, sg. n. *cosin*, pl. *cosna, cusna* 12

co, co n-, con, conn, conj. 'that,' 'so that'; *cen co* 'without that'; *co-n na* 'so that...not'; freq. combined with preverbal particles; *coro-, cor-, corr-* etc.; cf. also *conid*

cocad, m. 'war,' 'warfare' 5

co-crích, f. 'confines,' 'boundary,' 'borderland,' 'marches'; dat. *issin chocrich* 14; acc. *in cocrích* 6, 9

cóica, m. 'fifty' 5

cóiced, m. 'a "fifth" part of Ireland,' 'a province'; sg. acc. *cóiced* 14; dual nom. *cóiced* 5

coich, interrog. pron. 'who' 10, 14

cóir, adj. 'proper,' 'just' 6

coire, cf. *core*

colainn, f. 'flesh,' 'body,' acc. 19

colluid, cf. *lod*

comairle, f. 'counsel' 3

comairlim, 'I take counsel'; imperf. sg. 3 *no chomairled* 3

com-ard, 'as high as,' 'of equal height' 18

com-máin, f. 'a counter-gift,' 'mutual favour,' 'obligation' 2 (here 'the same amount')

com-méit, n. 'an equal size or quantity' 2

com-ram, m. 'strife,' 'contest,' 'triumph,' 'trophy' 11; dat. (*do*) *chomram* 10, 12; acc. *comram* 16; gen. *chomraime* 16, pl. dat. *chomramaib* 6

comtaig? Windisch connects w. *cómthach* 'a companion'

co n-accatar, cf. *adcíu*

concelim, 'I conceal'; pass. pres. sg. 3 *concelar* 3

conid, 'so that it is'; *co-n* (conj. 'that,' 'so that') + *-id* (3rd sing. conjunct. form of the copula). Cf. ch. 3, note s.v.

conna (co-n na), 'so that not'

córa, córe, f. 'peace,' 'right relationship,' 'fitness'; sg. dat. *i córai* 14

core, f. 'a caldron'; sg. dat. *coire* 1, acc. *coire* 1, pl. n. *core* 1

cor-rala, cf. *-lá*

cor-ralsat, cf. *-lá*

cor-ranic, cf. *riccim*

cor-riacht, cf. *riacht*

cor-roimid, cf. *maidim*

coss, f. 'foot'; in cpd. acc. *oen-chois* 12; dual acc. *cois* 18

costud, m. (1) 'restraining,' 'checking'; (2) 'custom,' 'usage,' 'habit' 17; cf. *droch-costud* 'evil custom' 17 (Meyer); 'to wrangle,' 'dispute' (O'Donovan, Suppl.)

cotlud, m. 'sleep'; sg. gen. *chotulta* 3, acc. *cotlud* 3

créchtach, 'wounded,' 'dealing wounds'; sing. gen. *crechtaig* 15

cret, f. 'chariot-framework'

crích, f. 'border,' 'boundary,' 'district'; sg. dat. *crích* 1

cride, n. 'heart' 15

criss, 'a girdle,' 'belt'; sg. dat., e.g. *assa chriss* 16

crothim, 'I shake'; s-pret. sg. 3 *crothiss*

crú, 'blood'; sg. dat. *chrú* 18

crúaid, 'hard,' 'hardy,' 'stern'

cú, m. 'a greyhound,' 'hound,' 'dog' 1 etc.; sg. gen. *con* 1 etc., acc. *coin* 4, pl. gen. *con*

cúairt, f. 'circle,' 'ring'; sg. acc. *cuairt*; verb. n. of *cúartaim* w. prep. *imm*, 'I surround'? 17

cucain-ni, cf. *co*

chuci-sium, cf. *co*

cuich, cf. *coich*

cuingid, 'demanding,' 'seeking' (for *cuindgid, condegid*), verb n. of *cuindigim, cuingim* sg. nom., e.g. *chungid* 16; sing. dat. *do chungid* 1, 2

cuit, 'portion,' 'share,' 'part' 15, 18 etc.

cúl, m. the 'back'; sg. *iar cúl* 20

cumma, 'equal' 3

cuntubart, f. 'doubt'; sg. dat. *cuntabairt* 4

cur, m. 'hero'; sg. gen. *curad* 15, pl. n. *curaid*

cusna, cf. *co*

cutal, 'empty,' 'at a loss,' 'resourceless' or 'feeble,' 'spiritless' 3

D.

dá, m. *di*, f. *dá* n- neut. 'two,' in compos. *dé-*; gen. *da* (without distinction of gender), dat. *dib*, acc. m. *dá*, f. *di*, n. *dá*; e.g. *etir cech da dorus* 5

dabar, cf. *damim*

dáine, cf. *dune*

dair, f. 'an oak'; sg. acc. *dair* 18

dairbre, 'an oak,' 'an oakwood'; sg. acc. *dairbre*

dálaim, 'make a tryst,' 'meet'; pres. indic. pl. 3 *ro-dalait-seom* 5

dam, m. 'an ox' 1; pl. gen. *dam* 6

dam-dabach, f. lit. 'a tub large enough to hold an ox'; fig. 'a cover or shelter of shields' (sc. like an ox-vat) 17

damim, 'I grant,' 'yield,' 'allow'; perf. dep. 3 *damair*; pass. pres. sg. 3 *dabar* (with aspirated *m* written phonetically as *b*) 6

dano, transition particle, 'also,' 'further,' 'now,' 'thereupon,' 'moreover' 9 etc.

dar, cf. *tar*

de, cf. *di*

-dechad, perf. of *tiagu*; 'I went,' 'I have gone'; sg. 3 *co n-dechaid* 13

deg-, dag-, 'good,' e.g. *deg-caratrad* 2 (cf. *caratrad*)

delb, f. 'shape,' 'form,' 'figure'; sg. dat. *ar deilb* 14

dénim, 'I make'; pres. sg. 3 *déni* 3; pass. subj. sg. 3 *dentar* 6

deoch, deog, f. 'drink'; sg. acc. *dig* 3

deod, n. 'end'; sg. dat. *fo deoid*, 'at last' 8, 12

derb, 'sure,' 'certain,' 3

desin, cf. *di*

dess, 'right,' 'southern,' *andes* 'from the south' 20

dessid, perf. (for *do-essid*) 'he sat down' 8, 9, 13, 16

di (de), prep. w. dat. 'of,' 'from.' In Middle Ir. confused w. *do* 'to'; combined w. the article *din*, *dind*, pl. *dina*; combined w. the pers. prons. sg. 1 *dim*, *dim-sa*, 3 *de*, *de-sium*; pl. 1 *dind*, 2 *díb*, 3 *díb*; combined w. the possess. prons. sg. 1 *dim*, 2 *dit*, 3 *dia*; pl. 1 *diar*, 3 *dia n-*; combined w. rel. pron. *dia n-*; takes the place of a partitive gen. w. nouns or pronouns 5

dia, see *di* and *do*

dia, 'a day,' 20; *dia bliadna* 'that day a year hence'; cf. *dia sechtmaine* 'that day week'; *dia mís* 'that day a month'

díblínaib (cf. *dá*, *lín*), 'to either side' 3

díburgun, 'a casting,' 'shooting' 17; cf. *díbairgim* 'I cast,' 'fling'; verb n. (1) *do chloendiburgun* 17; (2) *diúbhracadh* 'shooting w. a bow'; pl. dat. *do cloin-dibraicthib* 17, Harl. 5280

dig, cf. *deoch*

din, conj. 'so,' 'now' 15, 16, 3

dind, 'pleasant,' 'beautiful,' 'delightful'; pl. n. *dind*

dítnaim, 'I protect,' 'shelter,' 'defend'; imperf. sg. 3 *no-ditned* 1

do, prep. w. dat. 'to,' often confused w. *di* q.v.; causes aspiration; vowel elides before a fol. vowel; combined w. article sing. *don* 17, pl. *dona*; combined w. the personal prons. sg. 1 *dam*, *dam-sa* 'to me,' 2 *duit*, *duit-siu* 'to you,' 3 m. and n. *dó*, *do*, f. *di*, *di*, pl. 1 *dún*, *dun*, 2 *dúib*, *duib*, 3 *dóib*; combined w. the possess. prons. sg. 1 *dom*, 2 *dot*, 3 *dia*, *dia*, pl. 1 *diar n-*, 2 *do bor n-*, 3 *dia n-*;

combined w. the rel. pron. (*an-*) *día n-*, *dia n-*; commonly used with verb. n. in idiom. constructions

do-, in compos., and w. infixed prons. *dom*, *dot* etc.; w. verbs alone *tánac* (for *to- anac*) 'I came'

do, du, pron. poss. 'thy'; if the *-o*, *-u* is elided before an initial vowel *d* appears as *t* or *th*, e.g. *th'athair* 12. In combination w. preps. the final vowel is lost and *d* appears as *t*, e.g. *dit*, *fort*, *triat*

dobertar, cf. *dobiur*

dobiur, 'I bring,' 'I give' (w. dat.); pres. sg. 2 *doberi-siu* 3 (but see note), *dos-beir* 3; imperf. sg. 3 *dobered* 1; fut. sg. 1 *dobér* 16, 3 *do-don-béra* 3; condit. sg. 3 *dobérad* 12, 13, 16; pass. pres. sg. 3 *doberar* 18; pass. fut. sg. 3 *doberthar* 2, pl. 3 *dobertar* 2

dochuadusa (for *dochuadus-sa*), perf. sg. 1, 'I went' 10, 2 *dochuadais* 14, *dochuadaisiu* 9

dodechaid, cf. *do-thiagaim*

dodnancatar, cf. *ticcim*

do-don-béra, cf. *dobiur*

do-faeth, 'will fall'; sg. 3 *do-faeth* 3. Cf. *tuitim*

do-gníu, 'I do,' 'make,' pres. sg. 3 *dogní* 5

dollécim, from do-lécim, 'I fling,' 'cast,' 'let loose,' pres. sg. 1 *dollécim-se* 11 (*do-n-leicim*, w. infixed pron.)

dollod, do-lod, 'I went,' pret. sg. 3 *dot luid* 13 (see note); pl. 3 *dollótar* (? for *do-n-lo-tar*, cf. *dollécim*)

don, do in, 'to the.' Cf. *do*

dona, cf. *do*

donáraill, 3 sg. pret. of *to-ad-ell*, 'he went at' 20

donarlaic, cf. *tar-laicim*

dond, cf. *do*

doraiga, cf. *togaim*

dorat (perfective of *dobiur*), 'he gave'; pret. sg. 1 *doratusa* (for *doratus-sa*) 4, 3 *dorat* 6, 14; pass. perf. sg. 3 *doratad* 17

do-rochim, 'I come,' 'reach'; pres. sg. 3 *do-roich* 10

do-roid, 3 sg. perf. of *do-fóidi*, 'sends along' 3

dorus, 'door'; sg. dat., e.g. *i n-dorus* 5, 11, pl. nom. *doruis* 1, acc. *dorsi* 18, dual acc. *dorus* 5

dosóim, 'I turn,' 'turn myself toward'; pres. sg. 3 *dosoi* 3

do-thíagaim, 'I come,' imperf. sg. 3 *do-theiged* 1; perf. sg. 3 *do-dechaid* 10, pl. 1 *do-dechammar-ni* 2

droch, 'wicked,' 'bad'; only in compos. *droch-daine* 17; cf. note s.v. *droch-costud* 17

dub, 'black'; gen. *duib*

dúib, cf. *do*

dun, cf. *do*

dune, duine, m. 'man'; gen. *duine* 16, pl. acc. (in compos.) *droch-dáine* 17

dús (for *do fíus*), 'in order to know' 19

E.

é, hé, sé, m.; **sí, í,** f.; **éd, héd,** n.; pl. **é, íat, síat,** in addition to the infixed and suffixed forms of the pron. of the 3rd pers. 'he,' 'she,' 'it,' 'they.' Combined w. preps. 3 sg. m., e.g. *oca* lit. 'at him' 1, *chuci-sium* 'to them' 1, *riss* 'to him' 3, *aire* 'upon them' 3, *inti* 'in it' (f.) 1, *tréthi* 'through it' (f.) 1, *impi* 'about it' (f.) 5, *doib* 'to them' 4, *leosom* 'with him' 5

écen, adj. 'necessary' 20

ech, m. 'horse'; gen. *eich*; pl. acc. *eocho* 9, dual nom. *ech* 2

ega, cf. *aig*

égem, f. 'cry,' 'clamour,' sg. dat. *fon égim* 11

eich, cf. *ech*

egim, 'I cry,' 'shriek'; pass. pres. sg. 3 *eigther,* pret. sg. 3 *ro héged* 11

eirr, cf. *err*

eocho, cf. *ech*

era, 'denial,' 'refusal' 3?

éraim, 'I refuse,' 2nd sing. pres. indic. *era-si* 3?

érbart, 'I have said' (for *as-ru-bart*), pret. of *asbiur*; pres. conj. pl. 3 *co n-erbrat* 20 for *as-ro-berat*

ere, aere, 'load,' 'burden' 17

érigim, 'I stand up'; imper. sg. 2 *eirg* 16

Ériu, f. 'Ireland'; gen. *Erenn* 5, 11, *Erend* 5, 6, 8

err, m. 'warrior' (fighting in a chariot) ? gen. sing. *eirr* 15

essara, cf. *esur*

esur, fut. dep. 'I shall eat'; sg. 2 *essara* 3

étaim, 'I get'; pres. indic. sg. 2 *etai* 14

eter, 'between,' 'among'; *et[ir]* 5, *eturro* 19 'between them'

etha, cf. *ethaim*

ethaim, 'I go,' 'find,' 'take'; pass. pret. sg. 3? *etha* 3

eturro, cf. *eter*

F.

fácabaim, fácbaim, 'I leave,' 'leave aside'; s-pret. sg. 2 *foracbaisiu* (for *fo-ro-ath-gabais-siu*) 7, *foracbais* 9, 14; sg. 3 *fargaib* 17; fut. pl. 3 *no con faicebat* 3; pass. pret. sg. 3 *foracbad* (for *fo-ro-ath-gabad*) 7; verb. n. *d'facbail* 7

-fachlisem (*ni ro-bar-fachlisem*), 'we did not expect you,' a late perf. of *fuciallathar,* 'expects' 5

fadéin, 'self'; with 2nd sing. 7

fagabar, cf. *fo-gabaim*

fáilte, f. 'joy,' 'welcome' 1, 4 etc.

fair, cf. *for*

fal-, 'a heap'?

far n-, 'your'

fargaib, cf. *fácabaim*

fecht, n. 'time,' 'occasion'; *a fecht-sa* 'now' 17; *fecht and* 'once' 10

féin, indecl. 'self.' *Tic-seom féin* 'he comes himself' 5

féith, f. 'sinew'; pl. acc. *féthi* 14

feithi 14 'sinews'

féne, ch. 3, cf. note s.v.

fer, m. 'a man'; sg. gen. *fir,* d. *dond fir,* acc. *dar fer* 15, pl. n. *fir,* gen. *fer* 6 etc., d. *feraib* 8, acc. *firu* 8

feraim, 'I pour,' 'give'; pres. pl. 3 *ferait* 15; pass. pret. sg. 3 *ro-ferad* 1

ferand, 'land'; sg. dat. *ferund* 12

ferdaigsecht, 'being steward,' 'waiting.' Cf. *ferthigsecht*

ferg, f. 'rage,' 'anger'; *ferg fene,* ? 'hero of the Fían' 3; sg. gen. *ferge* 15

fern, 'a shield'; sg. acc. *fern*

ferr, 'better' 7, 10, 16; 'best' 2

fertas, 'shaft of a chariot,' 'pole'; sing. acc. *fertais* 19

ferthigis, 'a steward'

ferthigsecht, m. 'waiting upon,' 'acting as steward'; sg. dat. *icond ferdaigsecht* 6

ferund, cf. *ferand*

fes, cf. *-fetar*

fess, f. 'feast'; sg. dat. *feiss* 2

fessin, indecl. 'self' 6

-fetar, 'I know' 10; pass. pret. sg. 3 *fes* (for *fess*) 3

fíadnaise, n. 'witness,' 'testimony'? 15

fiche, 'twenty'; pl. n. *fichit* 2, 5

fid, m. 'wood'; sg. acc. *fid* 20

fidnaisi, cf. *fíadnaise*

fil, 'it is,' 'there is,' 'he is' 16; pl. 3 *in fuilet* 12; cf. *-táu*

find, 'white,' 'true,' 'good'; Meyer 'fair'; Thurneysen 'schön'

fír, adj. 'true,' 'just,' 'right,' 9, 10, 11, 15, 16

fiand, 'red,' 'blood' 15

fled, f. 'feast'; sg. acc. *fleid* 5

fo, prep. w. dat. and acc. 'under'; combined w. possess. pron. sg. 1 *fóm* 16; w. the article dat. *fón* 9; in the sense of 'on the occasion of,' e.g. *tanacaisiu fon égim* 'thou camest at that uproar' 11; written phonetically *a* in *a chét-óir* 2

fochen, 'welcome,' 15, 4; cf. note s.v. *mo chen* 5, 6

focul, 'word' 14

fo-dáilim, 'I divide,' pret. sg. 3 *forodail*

fo deoid, cf. *deod*

fo-egim, 'I cry out'; pass. pret. sg. 3 *foheged* 13 (impers.)

fo-gabaim, 'I find'; pass. imper. sg. 3 *fagabar* 8

follaigim, 'I neglect'; pass. pret. sg. 3 *follaiged* 5

for, prep. w. dat. and acc. 'on,' ' over,' 'above'; used in idiomatic sense in 3, 8; combined w. the article, e.g. sg. dat. *forsind*; pl. *forsna* 18; combined w. pers. prons. sg. 1 *form*, 2 *fort*, 3 acc m. and n. *foir, fair*, f. *forrae*, dat. *fuiri*; w. poss. pron. *fort* 14

foracbad, cf. *fácabaim*

foracbaim, cf. *fácabaim*

for-gránna, 'very odious' 13

formna, 'multitude,' 'host,' 'band' 4

for n-, far, *bar* 5, possess. pron. 'your'; cf. *bar*

forsna, cf. *for*

fota, 'long' 3

fráech, 'heather,' 'heath'; sg. acc. *fraech* 20

fráech-red, 'heath'; sg. dat. *fraech-rud* 20

fraig, 'wall'; sg. acc. *fraig* 3

frecra, n. 'answer' 3

frem, 'root'; pl. dat. *fremaib* 18

fri (originally *frith*, traces of which linger in the compositional forms), prep. w. acc. 'opposite,' 'against,' (like) 'to,' (along) 'with,' (part) 'with'; combined w. rel. pron. *fris rater* (for *frissa*) 20; w. pers. prons. sg. 1 *frim-sa* 8, 10, 2 *frit* 14, 3 m. and n. *riss* 3; pl. 3 *friu* 1; combined w. possess. prons. sg. 3 *fria*

frith, 'was found,' pret. pass. 3 sg. 17. Cf. *fúar*

frithailim, 'I attend,' 'minister'; imper. pl. 2 *frithalid* 12

friu, see *fri*

fuachtnaigim, 'I quarrel,' 'attack,' 'injure'; pret. sg. 3 *ro fuachtnaig* 5

fúal, 'urine'; sg. gen. *fuail* 13

fúar, perf. 'I found'; sg. 3 *fúair* 12; pass. pret. sg. 3 *frith* 17

fúargaib, cf. *túar-gabim*

fuil, f. 'blood' 18; gen. *fola*; *a loim fola* 16

fuilet, cf. *fil*

G.

gabáil, cf. *gabaim*

gabaim, 'I take,' 'seize'; pres. sg. 3 *gebid* 17, rel. *gaibes* 9; pret. sg. 1 *ra gabus* 16, 3 *ro-gab* 8, 16; *ra-gaib* 20, *gabais* 18; dat. verb. n. *gabáil* 1, 20

gabor, gabur, m. 'horse.' Dual nom. *da gab[air]* 20

gai, m. 'spear' 14, 9; dat. *gai* 10; sg. acc. *gai* 11, *gae* 13

gairmim, 'I call,' 'shout'; pass. pres. pl. 3 *gairmter* 4

gal, f. 'bravery,' 'valour'; pl. 'brave deeds'; sg.gen. *gaile*, pl. dat. *galaib* 6

galar, n. 'illness'; sg. dat. *galur* 13

gall, 'a foreigner,' 'stranger'

gamnach, 'a milking-cow w. a year-old calf'; pl. gen. *gamnach* 5

gasced, (1) 'weapons,' (2) 'valour'; sg. dat. *-gasciud* 14; acc. *gaisced* 9, *gasced* 8; pl. dat. *gaiscedaib* 8

gein, n. 'birth'; dat., e.g. *ria ṅ-gein* 5

gíall, 'a hostage'

gilla, m. 'a youth,' 'young man,' 14; sg. voc. *a gillai* 14, pl. nom. *gillai* 6, 7, voc. *a gillu*

glanaim, 'I cleanse'; pret. sg. 3 *ro-glan* 12

-glé, ? pret. sg. 3 *ro-glé*, 'it became clear,' ? 4

gliad, 'battle,' ' strife'; *lond-gliaid* 15

gním, m. 'deed' 3

gó, f. 'falsehood,' 'guile' ? 12. See note

granna, 'hateful'; *for-gránna* 13

grith, 'shout,' 'noise,' 'uproar'; sg. acc. *grith* 18

guin, n. 'wound'; sg. acc. *guin* 16

gus, 'weight,' 'force,' 'strength' 15

H.

For forms beginning with *h* see under the second letter of the word

I.

.i., an abridged form, common in MSS, for Latin *id est* 'that is,' 'viz.'

-i, pronom. suffix, 3 sg. m. dat. and acc.

í, hí, pers. pron. 3 sg. f.

i, i n-, prep. w. dat. 'in'; w. acc. 'into';
combined w. article *isin* 5, 9, dat.
isind, acc. m. and f. *issin* 5, n. *issa-
n*, *is* 15 (w. loss of *a*); combined w.
pers. prons. sg. 3 acc. m. and n.
ind, f. *inti* 1, 9; combined w. possess.
prons. sg. 3 m. f. n. '*na* 2, pl. 1
inar n- 15; 2 *in far n-* 9

iarmairt 'issue,' 'result' 3, 15?

íar n-, prep. w. dat. 'along,' 'after';
combined w. article *iarsin* 1; w.
demonstr. pron. *iarsin* 4

íarom, íarum, adv. 'thereupon,' 'then'
5, 6 etc.

iarsin, cf. *iar*

íarthar, 'the western part,' 'the west';
sg. dat. *i n-iarthor* 1

ic, cf. *oc*

icond, cf. *oc*

il, adj. 'much'

ilar, n. 'multitude,' 'host'; sg. gen.
ilair

im, 'around.' Cf. *imm*

imbárach, 'tomorrow'

imda, f. 'bed,' 'couch' (Windisch);
'bedroom' (Stokes); sg. dat. *imdai*
2, 10, pl. gen. *imdad* 5

imm, prep. w. acc. 'about'; combined
w. the article and w. the pers. pron.
sg. 1 *immum-sa* 11; sg. 3 *immi* 3,
impi 5; *im fleid* 'at a feast' 5

immach, 'out of the house' 5, 18 etc.

imma-tarraid dún inti (impers.), 'we
encountered'? 9, 14; cf. *táraill* and
tarraid

imm-chomrac, 'encounter'; sg. dat.
im-chomruic 15

immorchor, verb. n. 'tossing' 3

immo-tarla, 'it came to this that' 8;
cf. *tarla*, and cf. note ad loc.

imm-scarad, m. 'separation,' 'separat-
ing'; sing. dat. *im-scarad* 15

imm-śnim, 'anxiety'; sg. dat. *imśnim*
4

imm-tharla, immo-tarla...dóib, 'it
happened to them' 8

imm-thigim (for -*thégim*, cf. *tiagu*),
'I go about'; pret. dep. sg. 3, *ro
im-thigitar* 6

immum, cf. *imm*

imorro, immorro, 'but' 5

im-scarad, cf. *imm-scarad*

im-snim, cf. *imm-śnim*

in, interrogative particle, 12, 15

in, ind, in t, an-, article, 'the'; the
original initial *s* is lost except in the
dat. and acc. after a prep. originally
ending in a consonant

indas, n. 'condition'; sg. acc. *fó n-*

innasin (for *innas-sin*), 'in this wise'
9, 14

indile, gen. 'cattle' 2

ingen, f. 'maiden,' 'daughter' 13; pl.
nom. *ingena* 20

innasin, cf. *indas*

inné, interrog. particle *in* + 3 pers. pron.
sing. m. *é* 12

innocht, adv. 'tonight,' 15

innossa, 'now'

inti, the article w. the deictic particle -*i*
before proper names, 3

inti, cf. *i*

is, copula pres. indic. sg. 3 absolute
form 1, 3, 4 etc.; 2 *at* 16. Conjunct.
form (with *con-*) *conid* 3, 14. Imper.
sg. 3 *bid* 4, *bad* 4. Subj. pres. sg. 3
(with *ce*) *cid* 3, and (with *ma*) *mad* 3,
16, (with *mani*) *manip* 3, 13. Future
absolute sg. 3 *bid* 15, rel. *bas* 2, 3.
Conjunct. sg. 3 *ba*, *ni ba fír* 9 ff.,
ni ba mór 20. Pret. absolute sg. 3
ba 3, 7, 12, 18, 20. Conjunct. forms
sg. 3 *nirbo* 5, 7, *corra-ba* 11; pl. 3;
niptar 5

isin, see *i* (prep.)

issed, i.e. *is* (3 sg. of copula) + *ed* (neut.
3rd sg. pers. pron.)

istaig, cf. *tech*

istech, cf. *tech*

itaat (*i* + *taat*), 'in which are,' cf. -*táu*

ithim, 'I eat'; imperf. sg. 3 *no-ithed* 1

L.

(ro)-lá, cf. -*lá*

la, le, prep. w. acc. 'with,' 'by'; combined w. art. sg. m. and f. *lasin*, n.
lasa; combined w. pers. prons. sg. 1,
lim-sa 3; 2 *latt* 20, 3 *leis* 4, pl. 1
lind 15, 2 *lib* 7, 3 *leo-som* 5; *la* is
also commonly used w. a noun or
pron. in the idiom. sense 'in the
opinion of,' e.g. 18 *la Connachta*,
'in the opinion of the men of Connaught'

laa, cf. *láthe*

-lá, 'threw,' 'lay,' 'placed,' 'sent'; suppl.
verb to *cuir* and *foceird*; pret. sg. 3 *ro-
lá* 3, 15, 19, 20, *ros-lá* 9, pl. 3 *ro lásat*
(*cor-ralsat*) *grith mór* 18; pass. imperf. 3 (*co*) *ro-lathea* 5

labraim, 'I talk,' 'speak'; pres. dep.
sg. 3 *labradar* 3

láech, m. 'hero,' 'warrior' 10; sg. acc.
laech 17; dat. *laech* 10, 16; in compos. *láich-cind* 12

lám, f. 'hand'; sg. dat. *láim* 15

lámaim, 'I venture'; imperf. pl. 3
laimtis 20

lán, 'full' 1

lár, 'floor,' 'ground'; sg. dat. *lár* 10; acc. *lár* 15

láth, m. 'hero'; pl. n. *láith* 6

láthe, lá, n. 'day' 3; sg. dat. *i n-oen ló* 5, sg. acc. *oen lá* 16, pl. acc. *laa* 4

-lathea, cf. *-lá*

latt, cf. *la*

lécim, 'I leave,' 'abandon,' 'let'; pres. sg. 3 w. infixed pron. *nos-leice* 16; pass. pret. sg. 3 *leiced* 19, verb. n. *lécud* 8

leis 3?

leith, cf. *leth*

lennán, 'darling,' 'sweetheart' 20

leoman, 'a lion'; ? *loman* 15

lerg, 'a raised plain'

les-anmannaib, cf. *less-ainm*

less, m. a 'court' or 'rath' enclosed by a wall or earthen rampart; sg. gen. *liss* 18; dat. *liss* 18, acc. *less* 5

less, 'advantage'; with *riccim*, 'profit,' 'emolument'; sg. acc. *les* 7

less-ainm, n. 'nickname'; pl. dat. *les-anmannaib* 12

leth, n. 'side,' 'half'; sg. dat. *leith*, e.g. *fo leith* 4, acc. *for leth* 19

lia, 'more' 3; compar. of *il*

lia, m. 'a stone'; sg. gen. *licce* 15

liasait, see *sliassit*

líath, 'grey' 13

licce, cf. *lia*

lilgach, 'a milch-cow' 2

lín, m. 'a number' ? 3

lind, n. 'drink'; *lind ocus biad* 'drink and food' 4

lind, cf. *la*

lingim, 'I spring'; pret. sg. 3 *ro-lĭng* 20

ló, cf. *láthe*

lod, 'I went'; pret. to *tiagu*; sg. 3 *luid* 4, 11, 13, 17, pl. 3 *lotar* 5; cf. *dollod*, *colluid* 11

log, 'fire'; sg. gen. *loga* 15

loimm, n. 'mouthful,' 'mass,' 'wave' 16

loitim, 'I harm'; sg. 3 *ro-loitt* 14

loman, cf. *leoman*

lomm, lom, 'bare'; sg. dat. *luim*? 3

lond, 'wild,' 'raging'; in compos. *londbruth* 15, *londgail* 3, *londgliaid* 15

lotar, cf. *lod*

lúaith, 'ash' ? 3 *lúath*

luchair, 'a glittering colour,' 'brightness' 15

luid, cf. *lod*

luim, cf. *lomm*

M.

m', cf. *mo*

-m, suffixed and infixed pron. of the first sing., cf. *mé*

má, ma, conj. 'if'

mac, 'boy,' 'youth,' 'son' 9; gen. sing. *mic* 5

macdacht, adj. 'marriageable' 20

macraille, 'testiculi' 13

mad (cf. *má*), 'if it be,' 'if it were,' 3rd sg. subjunctive of the copula with *má* 'if' 16

mag, n. 'plain'; pl. dat. *maigib* 19

magen, f. ? 'great' 15

maidim, 'I break' (intr.); impers. w. *for*; pl. 3 *maidit* 18; perf. sg. 3 *corroimid* 16, impers. *ro-mebaid* 19; verb. n. *maidm*, n. 'a breaking,' 'flight'; w. possess. pron. pl. 3 *ammaidm*, 'their flight' 20

máin, f. 'treasure' 3

mairfider, cf. *marbaim*

maith, 'good' 3, 4, 6, 14; pl. gen. *mathe* 4

mani, 'if not,' 'unless' 3; w. 3rd sg. imperf. 1

manip, 'if not' (*mani* combined w. 3rd sg. subj. of copula) 3

marbaim, 'I kill,' 'slay'; pass. pres. sg. 3 *marbthair* 5, pass. fut. sg. 3 *mairbfidir*, *mairfider* 6; verb. n. dat. *do marbad* 7

mé, pers. pron. 'I,' often combined with particle *se*, *mése*, *mésse*, *méisse*

mebaid, cf. *maidim*

mend, cf. *menn*

menic, 'frequently,' 'often' 7

menma, 'the mind' 3

menn, 'clear' ? 15

messe, cf. *mé*

messo, messa, 'worse,' compar. of *olc*; *ni messo* 2

méth, 'fat' 7

méthiu, 'fatter,' compar. of *méth* 7

mnái, cf. *ben*

mo, possess. pron. 'my,' aspirates the initial letter of the foll. word; combined w. a prep. *dom* 13, *fom* 16, *im* 16 etc.

mó, 'bigger,' 'greater,' compar. of *mór* 3

mochen, 'welcome' 5, 6; cf. note ad loc.

mod, 'astonishment,' 'concern,' 'attention' 3

mogda 3, cf. note

mol, 'a beam,' 'mill-shaft'; sg. acc. *mol* 18

mór, 'big,' 'great'; neut. *mór* followed by the gen. or *do*; gen. m. n. *móir*,

f. *móri*; dat. m. n. *mór*, f. *móir*;
acc. m. n. *mór*, f. *móir*; pl. nom. m.
f. n. *móra*

motha, cf. *cenmotha*

mucc, f. 'pig'; sg. gen. *mucce* 9,
muicce 15, *mucci* 8 etc., dat. *muicc*
8 etc., acc. *muicc* 9; pl. nom. *mucca* 6

mug, m. 'slave,' 'servant'; sg. dat.
mug 3

muinter, f. 'family,' 'company'; sg.
gen. *muntire* 14

N.

'na, na, cf. *in*

na, cf. *no*

ná, na, 'not' in relative and dependent
sentences; cf. *conna fargaib ní de* 17

ná, after the compar. for E. Ir. *indá,*
andá 'than'? 3

nach, 'not,' in dependent sentences
can generally be translated by 'that
not' 16

nád, 'not,' in dependent sentences

nammuicce, cf. *in* (article), *mucc*

neblai? 3

nech, 'someone,' 'anyone'; sg. acc.
nech 3, gen. *neich* 3

neim, 'poison'; sing. acc. *tri neim* 5

ni, dependent pron. pers. 'we'; -*ni*
suffixed, e.g. *do-dechammar-ni* 2,
cucain-ni 9, *dún* 4, *lind* 15, *ocain-ni*
7; infixed, e.g. *dodn-ancatar* 4

ní, ni, nicon (3) 'not,' negative of principal clause. *ní* aspirates the initial
letter of the following word; w. infixed pron. sg. 1 *ní-m* 3; sg. 3 *ní-s* 9,
12; combined with *ro* it becomes
nír 5; with *bo, ba* it becomes *níb*; cf.
niptar (for *ní batar*) 5

ní, n. 'thing' 3, 17

ninni, ? pron. 1 pl. used after *is* 3

no, untranslatable aspirating verbal
particle; used to infix prons., cf.
notes passim. Also prefixed to all persons of simple verbs in the imperfect
indic., past subj., and sec. fut.
tenses, and used in some parts of
the verb in a rel. function

no (for *nó*), 'or' 3, 11, 13

nóna, Lat. 'nona'; *cech nóna* 'every
evening'

nónbur, m. 'nine men'; gen. *nónbair*
17

O.

ó, 'ear'; sing. acc. 18

ó, prep. w. dat. 'from'; combined w.
the article, e.g. *ón taib* 3, *ón muicc*
16, *ond uair* 13; combined w. pers.
pron., 1 *úaim* 12, *uaim-se* 12, 2 *úait*

11, 3 *uad*; combined w. relative, *o
tucad* 3

ó, conj. (aspirating) 'since' (i.e. 'from
the time that') foll. by pret.; 'after'
foll. by perf.

óac, óc, 'young,' 'a youth,' 'a fighting
man'; voc. *a ócu* 5

oc, prep. w. dat. 'at,' 'by';
combined w. the article *ocon* 8, *icond*
6; combined w. pers. pron. sg. 1
acum-sa 7; sg. 3 m. *oca* 1, f. *aicce*
16; pl. 1 *ocain-ni* 7, 2 *acaib* 9; to
indicate possession *oc* is used with
the dative of the person and the
subst. verb, e.g. *bui cú oca* 'he had
a hound' 1; with the dative of the
verb. n. and the subst. verb expressed or understood *oc* is used in the
sense of 'to be occupied doing something,' e.g. *Mac Dathó fessin icond
ferdaigsecht* 6; with the dative of
the verb. n. of some verbs *oc* is used
to express the occasion on which an
action or event takes place, e.g. *oc
cotlud* 'during sleep,' 'while I slept'
16; *oc tabairt* 'while I took' 11

oca, cf. *oc*

ocu, cf. *óac*

ocus, conj. 'and'

óege, m. 'guest,' 'visitor'; pl. dat.
haigedaib 4

óen, áen, 'one'; indecl. or used in
compos. w. dat., e.g. *co n-óen-súil*
11, *i n-oen-ló* 5, *i n-oen-uair* 1; acc.
oen-chomram 16; w. the article 'the
same'

oenchois, cf. *coss*

oenchossid, 'one-legged'; sg. gen.
mac ind oenchoisseda 12

óinfer, 'single' or 'unique man,' indi-
vidual as opposed to a number 8

óentaim, 'unmarried'; pl. n. *mná
oentama* 20

óg-ríar, 'complete wish' 20

óir, cf. *ór*

ol, 'he said,' cf. *ar*

olc, adj. 'evil,' 3

oll, 'great,' 'grand'

ón, pron. dem. 'that' 17, 20

ón (*ó + in*), cf. *ó*

ond, cf. *ó*

ór, 'gold'; sg. gen. *óir* 20

ór, f. 'time,' 'hour'; *ond uair sin*
'since,' 'since that time,' 'ever
since'; *fo chet-óir* 'instantly' 13;
a chétóir 'at once,' 'now' 2, cf.
fo

orcain, f. 'destruction,' 'plundering'

ós, úas, adv. and prep. w. dat. 'above'
8

R.

ra- for *ro*, e.g. *cor-rala*, 19

ra for *fria*, e.g. *ra sliss* 18

rád, 'saying,' 'speaking'

rádim, 'I say,' 'counsel'; pret. sg. 3 *ro-ráid* 3, pl. 3 *ro-raidset* 2; pass. pres. sg. 3 *rater* 20

raidset, cf. *rádim*

rainnfither, cf. *rannaim*

rannaim, 'I divide'; pres. sg. 3 *nod-ranna* 15; rel., e.g. *cia rannas dúib* 15; fut. sg. 2, e.g. *nis-raindfe* 12; passive fut. sg. 3, e.g. *cinnas rainn-fither* 6; verb n. *rann*, *rand*, 'dividing'; sg. dat. *arraind* 6, 11; sg. dat. *do raind* 8 etc.

rath, n. 'favour,' 'sake' ? 3

ráth, ráith, 'a residence fortified by an earthen rampart'; sg. acc. *rath* 20

ré n, ría n-, prep. w. dat. or acc. 'before'; e.g. *ria ṅ-gein* 5; combined w. the article *riasin* 2

reílgis, cf. *teilcim*

rí, m. 'king' 1, 11; sg. gen. *ríg* 14

riacht (t-pret. of *riccim*), 'came,' 'arrived at,' 'reached'; sg. 3, e.g. *cor-riacht* 18; cf. note s.v.

ríam, adv. 'before,' 'earlier' 6, 11

ríar, f. 'will,' 'wish' 20

riasin, cf. *ré*

riccim, 'I come'; b-fut. pass. pl. 3 *ricfaiter* 7?, perf. sg. 3 *cor-ránic* 17

riss, cf. *ṛri*

ro, preverbal particle, aspirating. It is used chiefly (1) to convert a pret. or narr. tense into a perf., e.g. *asbert* 'he said,' *asrubert* 'he has said,' tho' the distinction is not clearly kept in Middle Irish; (2) attached to the present tense to give a perfect sense in general sentences; (3) to give a sense of possibility, e.g. *rolínad* 'he was able to fill'; (4) with the subjunctive (*a*) in wishes, and (*b*) after *acht, con, resiu*

rod-dét, pret. pass. of *damaim*, 'I grant,' w. infixed pron. 15

roichim, 'I reach,' 'come'; pres. sg. 3 *do-roich* 10?

ro-lá. The form *ro-lá* 'he threw' serves as pret. of *foceird*, the usual verb 'he throws,' and of *cuir*

rombertaigedar, cf. *bertaigim*

rota ? 7

roth, m. 'a wheel'; sg. acc. *roth* 9

ruccaim (for **ro uccaim**), 'I bring,' 'bear'; pret. sg. 3 *ruc* 12; pass.

pret. sg. 3 *no co rucad* 13; pl. 3 *ructha* 'they were brought' 1, 2

ructha, cf. *ruccaim*

rún, f. 'secret' 3

rúss, rús, 'knowledge'; from *ro-ḟius* 19

S.

-s, infixed pron., 3 sg. f., 3 pl.

-sa, demonstrative particle placed immediately after the noun, e.g. *fecht-sa* 17

-sa, enclitic emphatic particle of sg. 1

saide, cf. *side*

sair, adv. 'eastwards' 10

sál, f. 'heel,' sg. acc. *sail* 12

samail, adj. 'equal' 6; also verb n. 'comparing'

scél, n. 'narrative,' 'story,' 'history'

scían, f. 'knife,' 15; sg. acc. *scín* 8

sciath, m. 'shield'; sg. dat. *sciath* 11

scín, cf. *scian*

-se, enclitic particle of the 1st sg. e.g. *ṅaim-se*, sometimes attached directly to the pronoun, sometimes to the verb, e.g. *dos-leicim-se* 10

sé, independent personal pron. 3rd sing. 'he'

sech, prep. w. acc. 'past,' 'beyond,' 'besides' 20

secht n-, 'seven' 1, 5

sein, cf. *sin*

seo, cf. *so*

sessed, 'sixth'; sg. nom. f. *in t-ṡessed bruiden* 1

sét, 'a jewel'; pl. gen. *sét* 2

-si, emphasising enclitic pron. sg. 3 f. and pl. 2

síar, adv. 'westwards' 20

side, pron. demonstr. referring back to something mentioned before; used after a verbal form in nom. m. *do-fúargaib side* 8, *dessid side* 9, *nir-bo ferr saide* 7; after the possess. pron. w. noun as enclitic *co a biathad-saide* 5

sin (**sein**), indecl. demonstr. pron. 'that,' e.g. *Oengus mac Lama Gabaid sin* 10; (1) independent, e.g. *Cen motha sin* 2; (2) following a pers. pron., e.g. *is í sein* 1; (3) after an article + noun, e.g. *in tan sin* 1

-siu, cf. *-su*

sliassit, 'thigh'; sg. acc., e.g. *triat liasait* 13 (i.e. *ṡliasait*)

slicht, 'track,' 'trace'; sg. dat. *for a slicht*

slige, 'road'; sg. dat., e.g. *iarsin t-ṡligi* 1, pl. nom. *sligeda* 1 (acc. form)

sliss, 'side'; sg. acc. *comard ra sliss* 18 (here, 'wall')

slóg, slúag, m. 'troop,' 'host,' 'army';
sg. gen. *sluaig* 8, pl. n. *slúaig* 3,
18
so, seo, demonstr. pronoun, 'this';
(1) used independently, e.g. *cia so*
12, *cuich seo* 14; (2) after a pers.
pron., e.g. *inné seo Munremur* 12;
(3) after the article with a noun,
e.g. *is taig seo* 15; (4) *and-so*, 'in
here,' e.g. *cia andso* 11, *coich andso*
10
sochaide, f. 'party,' 'host,' 'band';
sochaide dib 5
sochraid, 'grand,' 'splendid,' 'beautiful'; adv. *co sochraid* 4
socht, 'silence'; sg. acc. *socht* 3, 9
sóim, 'I turn'; condit. sg. 3 *co suifed*
18
-som, common emphasising and con-
trasting enclitic particle of 3rd m.
and n. sg. and 3 pl. of all genders
(*si* in f. sg.); written *seom* or *sium*
after *i*. It is used after the 3rd
sg. pron., e.g. *do-som* 10, *chuci-sium*
1, 2; and the 3rd pl. pron. *leo-som*
5, *doib-sium* 3; after a verbal form
of pl. 3 *asberat-som* 19, *ro-dalait-
seom* 5
són, dem. pron. 'that,' e.g. *rot-bia son*
14
srón, f. 'nose'; sg. acc. *sróin* 6
sruth, 'stream'; pl. n. *srotha* 18
-su, -so, enclitic particle of 2nd sg.,
becomes *-siu, -seo* after a preceding
palatal vowel, and later becomes *-si*.
tusso 15, *chucut-su* 13, *duit-siu* 11;
combined w. a noun preceded by
possess. pron. *do menma-su* 3, *for
th' athair-siu* 10; combined w. verbal form in sg. 2 *atbertha-su* 3,
doberi-siu 3, *foracbai-siu* 7, *dochuadaisiu* 9, *tanacaisiu* 11 (for-*aig-siu*)
súas, adv. 'up,' 'upwards,' e.g. *atracht
suas* 4
súgim, 'I suck'; *ra-suig in tairr*
17
suide, neut. 'seat'; sg. acc. *suide* 10
suide, dem. pron. 'that'; *i suidiu,*
'then,' 'thereupon' 18
súil, f. 'eye'; sg. dat. *súil* 11

T.

tá, cf. *-táu*
tabairt, tabart, cf. *tabraim*
tabrad, cf. *tabraim*
tabraim (from *to-berim*, cf. *do-biur*),
'I bring,' 'offer,' 'give'; imper. sg.
2 *tabair* 3; imperf. sg. 3 *tabrad* 1;
verb. n. dat. *do thabairt* 2, *oc tabairt*
11, *ic tabairt* 16

tadall, 'visit'; sg. dat., e.g. *don chét-
tadall* 1
táib, cf. *tóeb*
taidlech, 'pleasant,' 'delightful'
taig, cf. *tech*
táin, 'cattle raid'; sg. gen. *tana* 11
tairec, 'attending upon,' 'supplying';
sg. dat. *do thairiuc* 15
tairissem (to-airissem), 'maintaining,'
'remaining'; gen. *laech a thairismi,*
'a hero who will keep it up' 17,
8?; dat. *do thairisem* 11
tair-lingim, 'to spring'; perf. sg. 3
tarblaing 15
taít, imper. 2 pl., 'come' 5
tallaim, 'I take away,' 'steal,' 'strike
out'; pret. sg. 1 *tall* 11
tan, f. 'time'; in adverbial phrase *in tan
sin* 1 'then,' 'at that time '; *in tan*
'when' 15
tanac, cf. *ticcim*
tancas, cf. *ticcim*
tancatar, cf. *ticcim*
tar, dar, prep. w. acc. 'across'; e.g.
dar sróin 6 etc.; used idiomatically,
e.g. *dar aiss* 'from behind' 20 and
cf. *fer dar fer* 15 note s.v.
táraill, 'he came'; cf. *donaraill*, gloss.
to *donarlaid*; cf. also *dom araill,*
Stokes, *Goid.,* p. 93 (42); *dotairaill*
etc.; cf. also s.v. *imma-tarraid* above
tarat, 'he gave' 3, 18; subj. sg. 2,
e.g. *ni thardda* 3
tarb, 'a bull' 15
tarblaing, cf. *tair-lingim*
tarla (from *to-rala*), 'it happened,';
cf. *immo-tarla*
tar-laicim (for *to-air-lécim*), 'I let
free,' 'let go from me,' 'cast'; pret.
sg. 3 *tarlaic* 10; *donarlaic* 20
tarr, f. 'hind quarters,' 'belly,' 'tail';
sg. gen. *tarra* 17; acc. *tairr* 17
tarraid, perf. 'hit,' 'lighted upon,'
'met'? 9
tarsnu?, 'relish,' 'condiment,' 'side-
dish'; *dia tarsnu* 6
-táu, substantive verb, pres. indic. sg.
1 conjunct. form: sg. 2 *no-tái* 3; 3
diata (prep.+rel.+*tá*) 10. Absolute
forms appear in sg. 3 *tathut* (*táth*
+suffixed pron. sg. 2); and in sg. 1
andó-sa 16, 2 *andaisiu* 10, 3 *andás* 7.
The absolute form prefixed by *ad*
appears in pres. indic. sg. 2 *atái* 13,
3 *atá* ?3, 16, 19; pl. 3 *atát* 6. As the
relative form the impersonal *fil* is
sometimes used, sg. *na fil* 16, also
after a conjunct. particle, sg. *ní fuilet*
12. Consuetudinal present, sg. 3 *bith*
3. Future absolute sg. 3 *biaid* 2. Con-

junct. sg. 3 (with infixed pron. sg. 2)
rot-bia 12, 13, 14; (with infixed pron.
pl. 3) *ros-bia* 4. Pret. absolute sg. 3
boí, buí 1; conjunct. sg. 1 *ro-bá* 4, 16,
sg. 3 *ro-bói* 1, 5, 17, 18, *ro-bái* 18, *cor-
rabi* 3, *co m-buí* 10 (with infixed pron.
sg. 1), (and 3) *ros-bói* 3; pl. 3 *co m-
bátar* 5, 18. Subj. past sg. 3 *no-beth*
16

tecat, cf. *ticcim*

tech, n. 'house' 5; sg. gen. *tigi* 5,
taige 15, 18, *thaige* 11; dat. *taig* 5,
15; acc. *thech* 3, *tech* 15. Used with
the prep. *in* after verbs of motion
expressed or implied, e.g. *con-accatar
C. C. istech* 'they saw C. C. (coming)
in' 15; also in dat. *istaig* 15

techt, 'going'; verbal noun of *ticcim*;
sg. dat. *do techt, ic techt* 20

techt, 'messenger'; pl. n. *techta* 2, 4,
dat. *tectaib*

teilcim, 'I let go from me,' 'cast,'
'throw'; pret. sg. 1 *ro-thelgiusa* 13,
2 *ro-thelgis* 11, *do-reilgis* 13

téit, teiti, 'he' 'it goes' 3; cf. *tiagu*

telgis, cf. *teilcim*

tellaige, cf. *tenlach*

tenlach, tellach, 'hearth'; pl. nom.
tellaige 1

tess-buith, 'to miss,' 'fail,' 'be lacking'; past subj. 3 *tesbad* 3

tess-tá (for *to-ess-tá*), 'there is lacking'; *atesta* (*a testa, a n-* rel.)
6

thaige, cf. *tech*

thardda, cf. *tarat*

theiged, cf. *tiagu*

thesbad, cf. *tess-buith*

thoetsat, cf. *tuitim*

thucad, cf. *tuccaim*

thuile, cf. *tol*

tíagu, 'I go'; impers. fut. sg. 3 *tiastar*
4; cf. *-dechad*

tíastar, cf. *tíagu*

ticcim (for *to-iccim*), 'I come'; pres.
sg. 3 *tic* 5; imper. pl. 3 *tecat* 4, 17;
perf. sg. 1 *tanac-sa* (for *to-anac-sa*)
13, 2 *tanacaisiu* (w. ending borrowed
fr. s-pret.) 11; 3 *tánic* 13, pl. 3 *dodn-
ancatar* 'who (pl.) have come to us'
(w. infixed pron. of pl. 1) 4, *tancatar*
1; pret. sg. 3 *tancas* (impers.) 1

tigi, cf. *tech*

tinne, 'a salted pig' 1

tír, n. 'land,' 'country'; sg. dat. e.g.
do thír 3, *isin tír* 11

tnúthach, 'jealous' ? 15

tó, túa, 'silent,' 'mute'; dual gen.,
e.g. ? *Mac Dathó* (? *dá thó*) 1 etc.

tóeb, n. 'side'; sg. dat. *táib* (*tóeb*) 3

togaim, 'I choose'; imper. sg. 2 *tog*
?20; condit. sg. 3 *no-thogad* 19;
perf. sg. 3 *do-róiga* 19

tóim (for *to-sóim*), 'I turn'; sg. 3 *dosoi* 3

toirchi 9? see note

tol, f. 'will,' 'wish'; sg. gen. *tuile* 2

tón, 'back'; *fó tóin* 7

tongu, 'I swear'; pres. sg. 1 *tongu*
16, pl. 3 *tongat* 16

trá, conj. 'now,' 'but,' 'therefore'
2 etc.

tráth, n. 'hour,' 'time,' 'period'; pl.
nom. *tráth* 3, 12

tré, tría, tri, prep. w. acc. 'through';
combined w. pers. prons. sg. 2 *triut*
9; 3 f. *tréthi* 1; combined w. possess.
prons. sg. 2 *trét chend* 11, *triat
liasait* 13, *triat bragit* 14

trebar, 'wise' 3

trén, 'strong' 15

tress, 'battle'; sing. gen. *tressa* 15

trethan, 'sea,' especially 'stormy sea'
15

tréthi, cf. *tré*

trí, 'three'; f. *tri fichit* 5, *tri cóicait*;
n. *tri chét* 5; acc. n. *tri thráth* 3, *tri
aidche* 4

trian, 'a third part'; sg. acc. *trian do
muntire* 14

triat, cf. *tré*

triut, cf. *tré*

troscim, 'I fast'; verb. n. nom. *in troscud* 3

truastad, verb. n. 'striking' 18

tú, 'thou'; with enclitic particle *tussu,
tusso* 15; combined w. prep. *duit* 16,
duit-siu 11, *frit* 14, *latt* 20

túarcim, 'I strike in pieces'; verb.
n. *túarcon*; dat. sg. *dom-thuarcain* 13
(with pron. 1st pers. sing.?). See note

túar-gabim (from *to-fo-ar-gabim*), 'I
raise,' 'raise up'; s-pret. sg. 3
do-fúargaib 8

túath, f. 'people,' 'tribe'; sg. acc.
dar sin túaith 3

tuccaim, 'I bring'; imperf. sg. 3 *thucad*
1; pret. sg. 1 *thucusa* 12; pass. pres.
sg. 3 *tucad* 3

tuile, cf. *tol*

tuitim, 'I fall'; fut. pl. 3 *thoetsat* (for
thoethsat, cf. H. 3. 18 *taethsat*) 3; 3
sg. s-fut. *dofaeth* 3

turbaid, f. The word is no doubt L.
turbatio and the meaning must therefore be 'disturbance'; *turbaid chotulta*, 'disturbed sleep,' 'sleeplessness'

turem, 'counting,' verb. n. of *do-rímim
lia turim* 3

tusso, cf. *tu*

U.

úachtar, óchtar, n. 'the upper part';
  sg. acc. *tria uachtur do macraille*
  13
uair, cf. *ór* ('hour')
uait, cf. *ó* (prep.)

úall, f. 'vanity,' 'pride'
úallach, 'proud' 4
úas, cf. *ós*
ule, 'all'; sg. acc. *forsin cóiced uile* 14;
  pl. n. *uili* 5; acc. *friu uile* 1
urchor, n. 'a cast'; acc. *urchor* 10

INDEX OF PROPER NAMES

The references are to English translations where possible, but in many of the sagas the text will be found printed on the opposite page. References to the *Táin Bó Cúalnge* are to Dunn's translation, *The Ancient Irish Epic Tale, 'Táin Bó Cúalnge,'* London, 1914. Reference is made to many of the stories mentioned in this index in the list of principal stories (*primscéla*) which are said to make up the repertoire of a file. This list occurs on fo. 151 *a* of the Book of Leinster and is printed by O'Curry in Appendix LXXXIX (p. 584 ff.) of his *Lectures on the MS Materials of Ancient Irish History* (Dublin, 1878). References to all the heroes mentioned below will be found in Thurneysen, *Die irische Helden- und Königsage* (Halle, 1921).

Ailbe 1, 19 'fair woman,' the name of Mac Dathó's hound; common also in place-names. For the finding of Ailbe and its presentation to Mac Dathó see the "Death of Celtchair mac Uthechair" transl. by K. Meyer in Royal Ir. Acad., Todd Lecture Series, vol. XIV, p. 24 f.

Ailill 1 etc.; gen. *Ail[il]la* 19, 20; dat. *Ailill* 3. King of Connaught, husband of Medb; a contemporary of Conchobar mac Nessa of Ulster and Curói mac Dári of West Munster. His rath was at Cruachan Ai in modern Co. Roscommon. It was in his reign that the *Táin Bó Cúalnge* took place. English transl. by J. Dunn (Nutt, London, 1914); L. W. Faraday, *Cattle-Raid of Cualnge* (London, 1904).

Anlúan 16, one of the Connaught heroes. It is stated that in the Book of Druim Snechta, a lost MS believed to date from the first half of the 8th century, after the death of Cormac Conloinges at Da Choca's (q.v.) hostel Anlón, son of Doiche, son of Maga, took his head to Athlone. See "Da Choca's Hostel," transl. Stokes, *Revue Celtique*, vol. XXI, p. 391. Cf. however Thurneysen *Die irische Helden- und Königsage*, p. 16 note.

Áth Luain 20, the modern equivalent is Athlone, on the borders of Co. Roscommon and West Meath.

Áth mac Lugnai 20, i.e. "Ford of the son of Lúghna" at Clonsast, King's County (Hogan), on the N.E. branch of the Gabhal—an inference derived no doubt from its position in relation to the other places on Ailbe's route. This ford is also mentioned in a poem by Dubhthach Ua Lugair in praise of Crimthann, a king of Leinster in the

fifth century. See O'Curry, "MS Materials," pp. 5, 486.

Áth Midbine 20 is mentioned in the story of the Great Battle of Mag Muirthemne. Cf. Thurneysen, *Irische Helden- und Königsage*, p. 556.

Belach Mugna 20, modern Bellaghmoon in the south of Co. Kildare.

Bile, i m-Biliu 20. The name occurs in the form *a Feraib Bili* in Rawl. B. 512. Meyer identifies with the barony of Farbill, Co. West Meath.

Blai briugu 1, mentioned in the poem on the hostels of Ireland. Cf. p. 5 above. The adventures of Celtchair mac Uthechair in his hostel and the subsequent death of Blai are related in "The Death of Celtchar mac Uthechair," in "The Death-Tales of Ulster Heroes," transl. Meyer, R.I.A. Todd Lecture Series, vol. XIV, p. 25 ff. Reference is probably made to some version of this tale in the "Tragical Death of Bla Briugad" mentioned in the list of principal stories (*primscéla*) in the Book of Leinster, fo. 151 *a* (see O'Curry, *MS Materials of Ancient Irish History*, p. 588 f.). Many of the other stories referred to in this appendix are mentioned in the same list.

Brefne 1, Co. Leitrim and Co. Cavan, cf. *Mac Dareo.*

Bricriu mac Carbaid 6, surnamed *Nemthenga* 'poison tongue.' He frequently appears in the Irish Sagas as a mischief maker, and inciter to combat. See especially *Bricriu's Feast*, ed. with transl. by G. Henderson (Irish Text Soc. 1899); *Táin Bó Cúalnge* (transl. Dunn), p. 169.

Cell Dara 20, modern Co. Kildare.

Celtchair mac Uth[echair] 7, 13, an

Ulster hero. Cf. the *Táin Bó Cúalnge*, p. 328. He figures as the owner of a magic spear in Da Derga's Hostel. The saga of his death is transl. by Meyer in "The Death-Tales of Ulster Heroes,"R.I.A. Todd Lecture Series, vol. xiv, p. 24 f., where he is said to have died from the touch of the blood of his dog Dóelchú.

Cet mac Matach pass. a hero in the following of Ailill and Medb, though of Munster family. The saga of his death in single combat with Conall Cernach is translated by Meyer in "The Death-Tales of Ulster Heroes," R.I.A. Todd Lecture Series, vol. xiv, p. 36 ff.

Conalaid 7. Unidentified, cf. note s.v. Can the *Luachair* here referred to be Slieve Logher, a mountain range dividing Limerick from Kerry and extending into Cork?

Conall Cernach 15, the greatest of the Ulster heroes of the older generation. He is frequently spoken of as being absent on long journeys and arriving home at the critical juncture, as here and also in "The Fate of the Children of Uisneach" (cf. s.v. *Conchobar*). Cf. *Táin Bó Cúalnge*, p. 336 f. The saga of his death is transl. by Meyer, *loc. cit.*

Conchobar mac Nessa, 1 etc., King of Ulster, and son of Cathbad the Druid. His seat was the Craob Ruad (the modern farm of Creeveroe), the House of the Red Branch at Emain Macha, q.v. He was ruling in Ulster when Ailill and Medb led the *Táin Bó Cúalnge* against him. He had previously displaced Fergus mac Roich (q.v.) from the kingship. Cf. s.v. *Ailill, Medb*. The story of his birth is translated by K. Meyer in the *Revue Celtique*, vol. vi, p. 173 ff., and the R.I.A. Todd Lecture Series, vol. xiv, p. 1 ff. respectively. For his death see E. Hull, *Cuchullin Saga*, p. 267 ff.; O'Curry, *MS Materials* etc., Appendix cxvi, p. 637 ff., cf. further Stokes, *Eriu*, vol. iv, p. 18 ff.

Conganchness mac Dedad 7. Uncle of Cúrói mac Dári (q.v.) For an account of his death see K. Meyer, "Death-Tales," p. 27. The Clanna Dedad was situated in the neighbourhood of Slieve Luachra. Cúrói mac Dári was at their head with his stronghold at Tara Luachra. They are a

heroic clan analogous to the Clanna Rudhraige of Ulster under Conchobar mac Nessa.

Connacht, one of the five chief provinces (fifths) of Ireland. Cf. *Lagin*. The seat of the rulers, Ailill and Medb, was at Cruachan Ai. Cf. *Ailill*. The form of the pl. gen. is *Connacht*, dat. *do Chonnacht*[*aib*] 18; acc. *Connachta*.

Crimthann nia Náir 3. In the Annals he appears as son of Lugaid Riab n-Derg, the friend of Cuchulainn. He is said to have married a supernatural being called Nár. A romantic account of him is given in the *Annals of the Four Masters* (ed. O'Donovan, Dublin, 1856), vol. i, p. 93. The years of his reign are given as 8 B.C. to A.D. 8. Cf. also Keating, *History* (I.T.S., vol. ii, p. 235). It is evident from the gnomic character of his utterance in our passage that he was regarded as a sage, at least in after times.

Cruachan, Ráth Cruachain, now Rathcroghan, Co. Roscommon, the royal seat of Ailill and Medb (q.v.). See *Annals of the Four Masters*, s.a. 1223. It is commonly referred to in the sagas as Cruachan Ai, a word of uncertain origin.

Cruachnaib Conalad 7. Cf. note s.v.

Cruachniu mac Rúadluim 7. Cf. note s.v.

Cualu in gen. *Cualand* 1, the south of the modern Co. Dublin and north of Co. Wicklow.

Cúrói mac Dári 7, a king of the *Clanna Dedad* in West Munster, husband of Bláthnat of the Isle of Man. She was in love with Cuchulainn and helped him to slay Cúrói and was herself slain by Ferchertne, Cúrói's faithful poet, in revenge for his master. His story is narrated in outline by Keating, *History* (I.T.S.), vol. ii, p. 223 f. Cf. also "Eulogy of Cúrói" in *Ériu*, vol. ii, part i, p. 1 ff.; "The Tragic Death of Cúrói," ib. p. 18 ff; "Brinna Ferchertne" in *Zeitschrift für celtische Philologie*, vol. iii, p. 41 ff. Cf. also "The Intoxication of the Ultonians," transl. Hennessy in Royal Ir. Acad., Todd Lecture Series, vol. i, part i.

Cúscraid mend Macha 14, a son of *Conchobar mac Nessa* q.v., fostered by Conall Cernach; mentioned in Conchobar's suite in *Bricriu's Feast*, ch.

12. Cf. also the "Siege of Howth," *Rev. Celt.* vol. VIII, p. 61; *Táin Bó Cúalnge*, p. 319.

Da Choca 1, a smith and the owner of the hostel in Sliab Malonn in East Connaught in which Cormac Conlonges and his suite were attacked by the men of Connaught as they journeyed from Cruachan Ai to Emain Macha to Cormac's coronation. Da Choca was also himself slain in the attack. See the story of the "Hostel of Da Choca," transl. Stokes, *Revue Celtique*, vol. XXI.

Da Derga 1, the owner of the *bruden* in Co. Dublin in which Conaire Mór, the son of Etarscél, was destroyed by Ingcél, an outlawed prince from Britain, and a band of Irish outlaws. Cf. the *Annals of Tigernach (Revue Celtique*, XVI, p. 405); Keating, vol. II, p. 232. His saga is transl. by Stokes, *Revue Celtique*, XXII. See further *Ériu*, vol. III, part I, p. 36 ff.

Drochet Cairpre 20, Drehid, near Carbery, Co. Kildare (Hogan).

Druim Da Maige 20, 'Hill of the two plains.' O'Donovan identifies this with Drumcaw in the barony of Coolestown, King's Co.; Hogan places near and s. of Co. Kildare. (See *Annals of the Four Masters*, s.a. 1556, p. 1543, note *m*.)

Echbél mac Dedad 7. Cf. *Táin Bó Cúalnge*, p. 329, where Errgé Echbél is among the Ulster heroes described by Fergus to Ailill. Cf. also *Bricriu's Feast*, ch. XII.

Emain Macha 20. Cf. *Conchobar, Ulad*; a large rath, now known as Navan Fort, about three miles north-west of the modern Armagh. See the "Death of the Sons of Uisneach," transl. Stokes, in *Irische Texte*, 2nd series (ed. Windisch, Leipzig, 1887); and the 17th C. text published by the Society for the Preservation of the Irish Language, Dublin, 1914. See the description and plan of the rath by H. d'Arbois de Jubainville in the *Revue Celtique*, vol. XVI, p. 1 ff.

Eogan mac Durthacht 11, one of the Ulster heroes. Cf. *Táin Bó Cúalnge*, p. 320. He it was who slew the sons of Uisneach. See *Oided mac nUisnig* (Windisch, *Ir. Texte* 2 Ser.). See also *Bricriu's Feast*, chs. 3, 4.

Ériu, 'Ireland' 1; gen. *na hErend, Erend* 5, *h-Erenn* 11, 5, 6, 8; dat. *i n-hErind* 1.

Falmag 3? Meyer and Thurneysen regard this as a poetic name for Ireland, i.e. the plain of Fál (cf. *Inis Fáil, Falga*, and cf. Henderson's ed. of *Bricriu's Feast*, p. 142). Cf. however note s.v.

Fergus mac Léte 7, king in South Ulster shortly before the time of Conchobar, according to most authorities. The home of his family is traditionally assigned to Dun Rury, Dundrum Castle, Co. Down, though he himself is generally associated with Emain Macha. His saga is translated by O'Grady in *Silva Gadelica*, vol. II, p. 262 ff., where his encounter with a sea-monster is related at length. He also plays a part as contemporary king in the "Martial Career of Conghal Cláiringhneach," transl. MacSweeney, Irish Texts Soc. His sword, known as the *Calad Colg*, became an heirloom. Cf. *Ferloga* below.

Fergus 18, i.e. *Fergus mac Roich*, King of Ulster, dethroned by Conchobar mac Nessa. After the death of the sons of Uisneach who were under his safe-conduct, he left Conchobar's court and spent the rest of his life at the court of Ailill and Medb at Cruachan. I am not clear on which side he is represented as fighting here, and his sympathies are always divided between Ulster and Connaught, though ostensibly on the side of the latter. He plays an important part in the *Táin Bó Cúalnge*.

Ferloga 19, 20, Ailill's charioteer and armourbearer. His name occurs also towards the close of the *Táin Bó Cúalnge* (cf. Dunn's transl. p. 352 f.) where he is represented as having charge of *Calad Colg*, Ailill's sword, which had belonged to Fergus mac Léte (q.v.).

Fernmag 11, Farney, in S. Monaghan. The name occurs in the *Táin Bó Cúalnge*, p. 320, where 'the stout-handed Fermag' (so MSS Stowe and H. 1, 13) is located in the north. See also Annals of Ulster, s.a. 1001.

Fid ñ-Gaible 20. Feegile in the parish of Clonsast, W. of Rathangan, King's Co. (Hogan). O'Curry refers to the fork of the two rivers which met near Clonsast.

Forgall Manach 1, the father of Émer, Cuchulainn's wife. See the "Wooing of Cuchullin" in E. Hull's *Cuchullin Saga*. His rath was at Lusk in Co. Dublin. He is referred to in a poem on the hostels of Ireland. Cf. p. 5 above. See also "Bricriu's Feast," chs. 3, 4 etc.

Lagin 1, 'the men of Leinster,' 'the province of Leinster,' one of the five chief divisions (fifths) of Ireland, the other four being Ulster, Connaught, Munster, and Meath, where the árd-rí or high-king ruled at Tara, at least in later times. Mac Dathó's court is thought to have been in the south of the present Co. Carlow. The form is pl. ; gen. *Laigen*, dat. *Laignib*, acc. *Lagniu, Laigniu.*

Loegaire 9, probably *Loegaire Buadach*, one of the Ulster heroes. Cf. *Táin Bó Cúalnge*, p. 321. In *Bricriu's Feast* and the *Courtship of Émer* he is associated closely with Cuchulainn and Conall Cernach. The saga of his death is translated by Meyer, "Death-Tales of Ulster Heroes," R.I.A. Todd Lecture Series, p. 22 ff.

Loth mór mac Fergusa maic Léti 7. I do not know who this can be unless he is the father of Cúr mac Dá Lót who was slain by Cuchulainn in the *Táin Bó Cúalnge*. See Windisch's ed. p. 288.

Luachair Dedad 7. Cf. note s.v. The Clan Dedad belonged to Munster. For Luachra cf. s.v. *Conalaid*, and s.v. *Conganchness mac Dedad.*

Lugaid mac Conrúi 7, i.e. Lugaid, son of Cúrói mac Dári, a king in Munster.

Mac Dareo 1, the keeper of the *bruden* in which the *Aithech Thuatha* or 'servile tribes' of Ireland massacred the three kings of the free tribes while they were feasting. The servile tribes had as their chief Cairbre, Cat-head, who is identified in this version with Mac Dareo himself, and who ruled Ireland after the massacre. The hostel was said to be situated in Brefne in Co. Leitrim, Connaught. Cf. a translation of the story by E. MacNeill, in the *New Ireland Review*, vol. xxvi, p. 99 f.; Keating, *History of Ireland*, vol. ii, p. 238 f.

Mac Dathó (?'son of two mutes'), identified with Mesroeda in ch. 3, *v.* 9. His brother was Mesgegra, King of Leinster (see the "Siege of Howth" transl. Stokes, *Revue Celtique*, vol. viii, p. 53). Cf. the passage from the Rennes *Dindsenchas* referred to on p. 5 above. The court of Mac Dathó was thought by O'Curry to have been situated in the southern extremity of the present Co. Carlow. He possessed one of the chief hostels of Ireland.

Mastiu 20? now Mullach Maisten or Mullaghmast, Co. Kildare.

Medb 1 etc. Queen of Connacht, wife of Ailill (q.v.) and the most prominent woman in the Irish Sagas. She led the *Táin Bó Cúalnge* against Ulster. Many stories relate to various episodes in her life. We may mention among others *Bricriu's Feast* (ed. and transl. Henderson, I.T.S.); "Battle of Rosnaree" (ed. and transl. K. Meyer, R.I.A. Todd Lecture Series, vol. iv); *Táin Bó Fraich* (transl. Leahy); *Mesca Ulad* (ed. and transl. Hennessy, R.I.A. Todd Lecture Series, vol. i). An account of her death is given in *Aided Medba Crúachan* (transl. K. Meyer, *Celtic Magazine*, March 1887, p. 212).

Mend mac Salcholcán 12, one of the Ulster heroes identified by Fergus to Ailill and Medb in the *Táin*, p. 330.

Mide, the smallest of the five chief divisions (fifths) (cf. *Lagin*), situated between *Uladh* and *Lagin*, with its chief ráth at Tara, ruled over by the árd-rí. Meath came into existence later than the other four provinces. It does not exist as a territorial unit in the *Táin Bó Cúalnge*, which only recognises four kingdoms. The foundation of Meath is ascribed to Tuathal Techtmar in Irish history.

Munremor mac Gergind 12, one of the heroes of the Ulster army, who is described by Mac Roth to Ailill and Medb in the *Táin Bó Cúalnge*, p. 321.

Oengus mac Láma Gábaid 10. An Ulster hero who plays a part in the *Táin Bó Cúalnge* and other sagas.

Ráith Imgain 20, modern Rathangan, Co. Kildare.

Róirin 20, Róirin, Reerin or Reelion, a hill in Co. Kildare.

Senlaech Arad 7. Cf. note s.v.

Temair Lochra 7, i.e. Tara-Luachra, probably in Sliabh-Luachra, somewhere in S.W. Ireland in the neighbourhood of Co. Kerry. Cf. Hennessy's introduction to *Mesca Ulad*, p. v (R.I.A. Todd Lecture Series, vol. I, part I).

Ulaid, one of the five chief divisions (fifths) of Ireland. Cf. *Laigin*, *Conchobar*. The Ulster stories of the Heroic Age relate only to a small portion (the south-eastern) of the Ulster of today. On the other hand the Ulster with which they deal stretches further south along the east coast. The form is pl.; gen. *Ulad*, dat. *Ultaib*, acc. *na hUltu* 3, 19, voc. *a Ulto*.